Routledge Revivals

Nigerian Studies

Nigerian Studies
or
The Religious and
Political System of the Yoruba

R. E. Dennett

First published in 1968 by Frank Cass and Company Limited by arrangement with Macmillan and Co., Limited

This edition first published in 2018 by Routledge
2 Park Square, Milton Park, Abingdon, Oxon, OX14 4RN
and by Routledge
52 Vanderbilt Avenue, New York, NY 10017, USA

Routledge is an imprint of the Taylor & Francis Group, an informa business

© 1968 Taylor & Francis

All rights reserved. No part of this book may be reprinted or reproduced or utilised in any form or by any electronic, mechanical, or other means, now known or hereafter invented, including photocopying and recording, or in any information storage or retrieval system, without permission in writing from the publishers.

Publisher's Note
The publisher has gone to great lengths to ensure the quality of this reprint but points out that some imperfections in the original copies may be apparent.

Disclaimer
The publisher has made every effort to trace copyright holders and welcomes correspondence from those they have been unable to contact.
A Library of Congress record exists under ISBN:

ISBN 13: 978-0-367-11040-6 (hbk)
ISBN 13: 978-0-367-11045-1 (pbk)
ISBN 13: 978-0-429-02445-0 (ebk)

CASS LIBRARY OF AFRICAN STUDIES

GENERAL STUDIES

No. 48

Editorial Adviser: JOHN RALPH WILLIS

FISHERMEN AND TRAP AT OLOKEMEJI.

[*Frontispiece.*

NIGERIAN STUDIES

OR

THE RELIGIOUS AND
POLITICAL SYSTEM OF THE YORUBA

R. E. DENNETT

FRANK CASS & CO. LTD.
1968

Published by
FRANK CASS AND COMPANY LIMITED
67 Great Russell Street, London WC1
by arrangement with Macmillan & Co. Ltd.

First edition	1910
New impression	1968

Printed in Great Britain by
Thomas Nelson (Printers) Ltd., London and Edinburgh

TO
BEATRICE DENNETT

PREFACE

ADMINISTRATORS and missionaries are often blamed for adopting methods of administration or evangelising which we all know are not suited to the uplifting of the negro race. Destructive criticism of such methods is easy, and in this case, where both parties have sincerely done their best, quite unnecessary. The construction of a correct native policy is much harder to build up, and it is a question whether we yet have sufficient data to work with any certainty. I have been very much struck with Dr. Arthur Keith's first series of Hunterian lectures on the "Anatomy and Relationships of the Negro and Negroid Races." There he expresses the opinion that before further progress can be made in anthropological investigation it will be necessary to revise our methods, substituting for the present empirical measurements others founded on a more certain and scientific basis.

In the following pages I have approached the study of the native from a philosophical (in the old-fashioned sense of the word) point of view.

One of the most hopeful signs of the times in Nigeria is that natives (who, by the way, owe their education to the missionaries) are beginning to look upon their native lore in a more serious light than their dear old masters did. Bishop Johnson gave us a little work on Yoruba paganism from which I quoted largely in *At the Back of the Black Man's Mind*. Bishop Phillips wrote a little book called *Ifa*. The Rev. Lijadu has given us *Ifa* and *Orunanila*. Mr. Sobo wrote Arofa odes or poems. Dr. Johnson has lectures on Yoruba history, and Mr. John O. George has written a short account of Yoruba history. Dr. Henry Carr, the Chancellor of the Diocese of Equatorial Africa, a native of Egbaland, is an author of many interesting papers and keys to mathematical works. Mr. Adesola is now engaged in writing a most interesting account of Yoruba Death and Burial Secret Societies, which are appearing in the *Nigerian Chronicle*. Mr. Johnson is the editor of this paper which is doing such good work in this direction. Then Mr. Williams and Mr. Jackson, both also Africans, are editors of the *Lagos Standard* and the *Lagos Record*. These papers can be seen in the Royal Colonial Institute. In other lines of life the colony has produced many distinguished natives, but I have only mentioned the above because I am now only dealing with literature. That an African colony, not yet fifty years old, should have produced in so short a time so many men distinguished in letters is a very hopeful sign for its future and speaks for itself.

I am indebted to so many for help in producing this little work that it is difficult for me to know how many to thank. Captain W. H. Beverley has kindly

PREFACE

supplied me with the little map which will at a glance show my readers where Yorubaland is.

Mr. H. Dodd took the photographs of the fishermen and hunters. A native photographer, Mr. Holm, has supplied the rest.

Dr. Henry Carr, who is at present in England, has gone through the proofs with me and corrected as many of my mistakes in spelling native names as he has been able, which adds very greatly to the value of the work.

As I have to leave for Africa without seeing the final proofs, Mr. T. A. Joyce has generously promised to undertake this arduous task for me.

And away yonder in Africa are many to whom my thanks are due for their hearty co-operation and patience, among whom are the Forest Rangers Taylor and Pellegrin, the priest or Babalawo, Oliyitan, the sons of Agbola and other chiefs.

CONTENTS

	PAGE
EXPLANATORY CHAPTER	1

CHAPTER I
A FEW NOTES ON THE HISTORY OF YORUBALAND 6

CHAPTER II
CREATION AND THE SACRED STONES AT IFE 17

CHAPTER III
DEATH, BURIAL, AND DEPARTED SPIRITS ORO, EGUNGUN, ETC. . 28

CHAPTER IV
THE FOUR GREAT ESTATES IN THE NATIVE FORM OF GOVERNMENT 60

CHAPTER V
JAKUTA. THE FOUR WINDS 65

CONTENTS

CHAPTER VI
ODUDUA AND THE FOUR DAYS OF THE WEEK 73

CHAPTER VII
OBATALA 81

CHAPTER VIII
IFA AND THE FOUR WALLS OF THE YORUBA KINGDOM . . 86

CHAPTER IX
ESHU 94

CHAPTER X
AGANJU, YEMOJA, THEIR OFFSPRING, AND THE OGBONI OR COUNCIL 97

CHAPTER XI
OLOKUN OLOSA AND FISHERMAN 106

CHAPTER XII
OGUN, OSHOWSI, AND THE HUNTER 116

CHAPTER XIII
SEASONS 130

CHAPTER XIV
OKE, OJO, AJESHALUGA, AND FARMING 140

CONTENTS

CHAPTER XV
ODUS OF IFA 147

CHAPTER XVI
SHANGO—OYA—OBA—OSHUN 156

CHAPTER XVII
LAND LAWS 195

CHAPTER XVIII
CONCLUSION 209

LIST OF ILLUSTRATIONS

FISHERMEN AND TRAP AT OLOKEMEJI	*Frontispiece*	
LAGOS TYPES	*To face page*	10
THE ALAKE AND SOME OF HIS OFFICIALS . .	} " "	14
THE LATE BALE OF IBADAN AND SOME OF HIS OFFICIALS		
STONES SACRED TO OGUN	*Page*	19
GROVES SACRED TO ORE, WIFE AND CHILD	"	20
IN ORE'S WIFE'S GROVE.	"	21
STONE CHAIR PRESENTED TO SIR W. MACGREGOR BY THE ONI OF IFE, NOW IN THE BRITISH MUSEUM	} *To face page*	23
A CHAIR MARKET AT BADAGRY, S. NIGERIA . .		
OPA ORANYAN AT IFE	*Page*	24
TREE PLANTED OVER GRAVE WHICH THUS BECOMES SACRED	*To face page*	28
MEMBERS OF A FUNERAL SECRET SOCIETY IN LAGOS CALLED ADAMORISHA, WEARING DRESSES SIMILAR TO THE EGUNGUN, EGUN . . .	} " "	32
"PORO" HOUSE		
AGBOLO'S SONS. GREAT NATIVE HUNTERS . .	" "	119
METEOROLOGICAL CHART	*Page*	131
SACRED CAVE AT ABEOKUTA	*To face page*	164

MAP

THE COLONY AND PROTECTORATE OF SOUTHERN NIGERIA, 1910 . . . . *End of Vol.*

NIGERIAN STUDIES

EXPLANATORY CHAPTER

In trying to impart one's ideas on a foreign people to one's readers, a great difficulty arises, *i.e.* the fact that for the most part one's public knows little or nothing about the surroundings of the natives about whom one is endeavouring to write. Well, it would take many volumes to describe fully so interesting a people as the Yoruba, even if one had the ability, so that I must leave those interested in this general branch of knowledge to others who have written on the country. Then I sometimes find it impossible to explain many foreign words that will keep suddenly cropping up, so that my collection of apparent facts at times resembles bits of a mosaic which the collector has to leave to his successor to put together. I take for granted that these pieces are very precious to those who are ever on the look out for something new that may throw light on the many problems that are still puzzling the thinking world, I do not hesitate therefore to mention them. In presenting this little work, then, it is to be understood that I am fully conscious of its faults, but I am fearful often to correct them lest in so doing I may spoil the native colouring and inculcate some erroneous idea that may be really foreign to the people whose mental outlook I am trying to illustrate.

A new name of a personage or a deity suddenly appears on the scene, and I know that my reader requires a far more accurate account of him than I or my informant can give him; well, all I can say is that it is in this sudden fashion that we who try to gather information in some foreign fields obtain it.

I know that this jumpy style, which one of my friends describes as "writing in seven league boots," is very irritating to the earnest student, and, I am very sorry for this also, and I wish to assure my reader that I have tried to say as much as possible about these sudden apparitions, either at the time of their coming on to the stage or in notes which refer to other places in the book where more is said about them.

All my information is drawn from native sources on the spot, the arrangement and order is not mine. The order is taken from the order of the Odus (palm nuts used in divination by the priests of Ifa)[1] as given to me by the babalawo (priest) Oli-yitan, and from the seasons.

There is one more difficulty that I may be able to clear away. In *At the Back of the Black Man's*

[1] Ifa is the name of the Yoruba oracular deity.

EXPLANATORY CHAPTER

Mind the formula given is 4 + 4 × 6 + 4 or 32 parts in all, that is forming one whole. Now among the Yoruba the formula is 4 + 2 × 6 or 16 parts. This is the pith of the work. Thus I commence the book by giving my reader a very short account of the history of the Yoruba as we know it as well as from a native point of view. I then take a legend of creation given to me by an old priestess called Oja through the mouth of a man called Togun. This takes me to a short account of the sacred stones at Ife the religious capital and cradle of the Yoruba people. As these stones are said to be men and women who on their death have turned to stone, I then say a few words about death and burial customs from which I find I cannot dissociate some secret societies. A consideration of these subjects points to the fact that the Yoruba have beatified their ancestors. This being a natural and so a general practice, there are in consequence thousands of such Orishas or deified spirits, all of which must be most interesting studies of family history. But a great philosopher called Ifa (who is mentioned in the story of creation as one of the four great deities) is said to have chosen 16 persons out of these different classes of people and formed them into a kind of council. These 16 had their 16 family Orishas[1] and thus we get at the number 32 and the formula of the Bavili and the Bini as shown in *At the Back of the Black Man's Mind*. Crawley, in *The Idea of the Soul*, writes "Frazer

[1] See note 1, page 12.

gives the following description based on Maspero and Wiedermann." Every man (Egyptian) has a soul, ka, which is his exact counterpart or double with the same features, the same gait, and even the same dress, as the man himself. Many of the monuments dating from the eighteenth century onwards, represent various kings appearing before divinities, while behind the king stands his soul or double as a little man with the king's features. In modern Egypt every child born has a djinnee companion born with it. It is an angel, but often hurts its protegé. It is an exact counterpart of the person himself, except that for male it is female and for female male. Something like this exists in the naming of the child's Orisha among the Yoruba and will be found in the chapter on marriage.

To continue, I give my reader what information I am able about these chosen Orisha and find that they are connected with certain occupations, *i.e.* those of fishing, hunting, marriage, planting, marketing, and construction. I find that the native form of Government official for Orisha coincides with the heavenly one and I give the lists of Officials and Orishas. Further, the meaning of the Odus in the order given are connected with the Categories of thought, which I have shown exist at the back of the black man's mind in the Congo and in Benin, *i.e.* those of water, earth, fire, germination or conception, reproduction or pregnancy, death and life.

EXPLANATORY CHAPTER

In my concluding chapter I suggest that the elements of native religious and social government are to be found in the black man's nervous system, which in my opinion responds to the will of the Almighty Architect of their Universe.

CHAPTER I

A FEW NOTES ON THE HISTORY OF YORUBALAND

Introductory Historical Remarks

FROM Dalzel's *History of Dahomey*, 1793, it would seem that Yorubaland about the year 1700 was under one King, or Alafin, who resided at Old Oyo[1] or Katunga. That this kingdom when united was a very powerful one is shown from the fact that until the year 1818 the Dahomi paid tribute to the Alafin of Oyo.

It is only from this date (1700), when the decadence of the Yoruba Kingdom had set in, that the native chroniclers can give us any definite knowledge of the Yoruba history. From this time we have a list of Alafins given to us.

1. Ajagbo.
2. Abiodun.
3. Arogangan; during whose reign his nephew Afonja raised an insurrection and so hurried on the downfall of the Kingdom.
4. Adebo.
5. Maku.

[1] Pronounced Awyaw.

6. An Interregnum during which the Obashorun or Prime Minister of the Alafin seems to have kept the State from actual ruin.
7. Majotu.
8. Amodo, about 1825.

About 1830 Lander visited Old Oyo, but between 1833 and 1835 the Mohammedans captured and destroyed the old town, and the Yoruba were obliged to found a new capital where Oyo now stands.

It was about this time also that the Egba declared their independence. They were finally driven out of the country that they, as a section of the Yoruba people, occupied, and in 1838 they founded their present capital, Abeokuta.

A chief called Lishabi is said to have led them to Abeokuta, and to show how near to the mythological period of their history we even now are I am able to give you the story of how Lishabi when defeated by the Dahomi descended into the earth.

How Lishabi descended into the Earth

Lishabi was a great warrior who lived at Ikija, Abeokuta. One day when there was a great battle between the Egba and Dahomi, and the Egba were put to flight and many killed, Lishabi was so ashamed that he would not return to Abeokuta, and so pointing his sword to the earth asked her to open. She opened and he went headlong into her depths. His sword is there to this day marking the place where he thrust it into the earth. His brass chain is also there; and if anyone begins to draw the chain out he can pull about 40 feet of it out of the ground, but then Lishabi pulls it back again. Many people have seen pigeons fly out of the place, they feed here and there, and then go back, so they know Lishabi has his house there. One man tried to make a farm there and started felling the bush, but he died, so now no one dares to farm in this place. And the people of Ikija go there yearly to worship him. They offer rams, goats, fowls, and yams to him.

By the year 1840 the seeds of dissension sown by Afonja had spread so rapidly that we find the proud Kingdom of the Yoruba people split up into a number of so-called independent states.

Illorin had been lost to the Alafin, and is now inhabited by a mixture of Hausa, Fulah, and Yoruba.

Ibadan, a semi-independent state, still recognises the Alafin and pays tribute yearly,

The Egba, a fine race of agriculturists, declare that they are quite independent, as also do the Ijebu, Ilesha, Ife, and Iketu (now in French territory).

From 1840 to 1886, when the British Government intervened as peace-maker, wars between these parts of the Yoruba people were constant. From that date until 1892 the peace-maker has had to punish the Ijebu and Egba for closing their trade roads.

In August 1861 Docemo ceded Lagos to the British. In 1863 Kosoko ceded Palma and Lekki, much to the disgust of the chief of Epe, who refused

THE HISTORY OF YORUBALAND

to cede his rights and was punished for it. And in the same year the chiefs of Badagry ceded their territory to the British.

Lagos became a great slaving port about the year 1815 when the King of Benin and a few other chiefs refused to allow slaves to be exported from their territories. The original inhabitants of Lagos were a mixture of Bini and Yoruba people. When it became a port of export for slaves, such slaves as became residents as labourers and servants of the slave dealers and merchants added their quota to the population; and when after 1861 it became a British colony many freed slaves from Sierra Leone and other parts, more especially Brazil, made their homes there.

The Colony of Lagos in 1863 rejoiced in a separate Government, but in 1866 with the other West Coast Settlements it was attached to Sierra Leone.

In 1874, after the Ashanti war, Lagos became part of the New Gold Coast Colony and in 1886 it became a distant Crown Colony, since when its progress has been phenomenal.

The formation of the Niger and adjacent territories into a Royal Charter Co. with Mr. (now Sir) G. Goldie as Deputy Governor, following the declaration of a Protectorate of the Niger Territories by the British Government in June 1885, is so well known a fact that the mere mention of the event is sufficient.

And I need only jog my reader's memory to call to his mind a knowledge of the time when that part of the West Coast which finally became S. Nigeria was more or less governed by Consuls resident in the

Island of Fernando Po, called by Burton the Foreign Office Grave.

The time came when the Foreign Office having worked up the "Raw Material" the finer processes of the Colonial Office were applied.

In 1889 I was present at a meeting in Calabar when the Special Commissioner Major (now Sir) Claude MacDonald interviewed the Chiefs, and on the 1st August 1891 the Oil Rivers commenced a new era under the title of the Oil Rivers Protectorate.

The Oil Rivers Protectorare became what is now known as Old Southern Nigeria while the rest of the Niger Protectorate became Northern Nigeria.

In 1906 Southern Nigeria and the Colony of Lagos and Protectorate were amalgamated, and the Colony of Lagos and Protectorate became the Western Province of what is to-day known as the Colony and Protectorate of Southern Nigeria.

The following notes refer chiefly to this Western Province, known generally as Yorubaland.

The Origin of the Seven Yoruba States

In "At the Back of the Black Man's Mind" I pointed out that the Congo was composed of a central Kingdom surrounded by other six states, also that each of these states was divided into seven provinces, six surrounding a seventh where the Fumu or Chief of the sub-Kingdom resided.

F.S., in the *Nigerian Chronicle*, in a paper entitled "A Chapter in the History of the Yoruba Country," writes :—" Yoruba is one of the seven countries or

LAGOS TYPE.　　[*Face p.* 10.

LAGOS TYPE.

states which the Hausa people term Bansa Bokoi (the vulgar seven) in contradistinction to Hausa Bokoi (the Hausa seven); the latter term is applied to the original Hausa states and the former to seven countries or states originating from the same races as the Hausa people, but which do not form part of the Hausa nation."

He goes on to say, " There can be little doubt that the Yoruba people are at least intimately connected with the Orientals. Their customs bear a remarkable resemblance to those of the races of Asia. Their vocabulary teems with words derived from some of the Semitic languages ; and there are many natives of Yorubaland to be found having features very much like those of Syrians or Arabians."

Most natives I have talked to on this subject are conscious of this origin from a superior race, and the marked superiority of the Yoruba people to their neighbours certainly points to something of the sort.

But many also are only too anxious to ignore the fact that the country was peopled by pagan Africans and that they are consequently in reality a mixed race among whom paganism persists.

Now these dear old pagans are said to have given the name of their Creator Odudua to the leader of the Bornu immigrants whose real name has been forgotten, and there is a legend that a Hausa Mussulman came to Ife, the religious capital of Yorubaland, and told them to " worship Allah." " He created the mountains, He created the lowlands, He created everything, He created us." But in a critcism by the editor of the *Nigerian Chronicle* the coming of the Mussulman must be placed at a much earlier date than that given by F.S., *i.e.* many years after the eleventh or twelfth century of the Christian Era.

It is possible, however, that Mussulman influence, at whatever date it first made its appearance, may have been the cause of the reorganisation of the religion of the pagan Yoruba. It was perhaps the means of putting Jakuta or Shango, the thunder and lightning God, in his place and the substituting of Olorun, the owner of heaven, for that great Orisha.[1]

To this time, then, the Yoruba pagan may owe, not the origin of his Orishas, but the order in which the greater ones have been handed down to the present generation.

Mr. George, in *Historical Notes on the Yoruba Country*, gives us another variant of the historical traditions of the Yoruba. Mr. George says:— "There are many traditions about the Yoruba Kingdom. We quote one which says that the Yoruba Kingdom was peopled by six brothers; that at the departure of their father to his home in the north, they left their mother, whose name was Omonide, and travelled downward. These formed six distinct kingdoms and are known to this day by the respective regal titles: Alake, Alaketu, Onisabe of Sabe, Onila of Ila, Oni Bini or Ibini or Benin, and Oloyo of Oyo. Some time after they migrated downwards, their mother hearing that they were settled decided to visit

[1] Orisha = deified departed one.

them. On leaving home, she took with her the piece of cloth, the band or Oja, with which she had secured them on her back when they were young, and the small pot, or Oru, in which she had prepared their infant drink. She thought that perhaps, as they had become Kings, they might ungratefully despise her, and she was ready to curse all and any of them that might do so. Accordingly, she went first to Alaketu [1] the eldest. She was received with all the honours of her position. She was pleased at this reception, and after remaining some time she went to visit the Alake, where she was similarly treated. She spent some time here purposing to visit her other children. Ultimately she fell ill and died.

"It is said that she, being pleased with her reception by the Alaketu, gave him on her departure the band or Oja with which she had secured her children . . . . She told him that the cloth was an important charm which possessed the power of good and ill; that good or evil will follow anyone according to his wish or utterance while he holds or puts on this cloth. It is said that one of the Kings of Ketu, who never would go out on any public occasion without having on this cloth, was once upbraided by his Chiefs for it, and was threatened to be driven away from the throne.

"An altercation ensued, during which he made certain imprecations which are said to be operating upon the country and people to this time. That since

---

[1] Most of the Ketu country is now French and so separated from the old Yoruba Kingdom.

he was disgraced for having on an old cloth, made brown by the dust of age, their country will ever be red and dust covered, and their garment be it ever so clean will appear and remain dirty."

"During Omonide's stay with the Alake of Abeokuta she gave him the small earthen pot or Oru in which she had always boiled infant drink for her children. She told him that that pot was a charm which had the power to establish himself and his brothers in their cities; that it was to be kept in memory of her, that she would often visit them and that the pot should not be removed from the watch-care of the Alake by any of his brothers. The Oru, a small earthen pot, is spoken of as being now in the care of the Alake and in the Egbas' former town, which is about twenty-five miles from Abeokuta. There it is adorned and venerated in respect of their dead mother up to the present. Kings of the Interior seek and invoke the aid of their dead mother Omonide or Iyamode before coronation.

"At the departure of the father, he gave to his youngest son Oloyo a small Ado or gourd receptacle into which he had put some ingredients together with common sand, as it might be of service to him and his brothers in their travels. It was of great use to them, for, when they travelled southwards, they met a large river which they determined to cross. They got into a canoe and pulled off; for a whole day no land was visible. The next day Oloyo remembered the gift of their father; he opened the

THE ALAKE AND SOME OF HIS OFFICIALS.

THE LATE BALE OF IBADAN AND SOME OF HIS OFFICIALS.

[*Face p.* 14.

small Ado and poured some of its contents into the river. Immediately dry land was visible. Hence he is said to be the 'land owner' .... The Yoruba Kingdom was once a great Power in West Africa. It had Dahomey, Hausa, Tapa, and many other important tribes and countries under its control.

"It lost its power through internecine wars, which, together with foreign invasions, brought about an entire disruption of the Yoruba Kingdom. The remains formed themselves into small towns, their once tributary towns, and these countries of course became independent.

"In these small towns the remnant of the Yoruba nation remained in peace for about two hundred and fifty years. After this another war broke out, which we are told began at Apomu, a market in the Ijebu Country. In this war the whole Yorubaland was laid waste, and from this the exportation of slaves from the Yoruba Countries commenced."

Mr. George describes how a General called Maye, the Balogun (or war chief) of Ife, with his Captains, Abe and Laboside, overran the whole of the Yoruba Country. He appears to have become a great slave raider.

At his death the whole nation was again scattered.

He continues : "These wars which have laid our country waste one hundred years ago, still continue from that time to this" (somewhere in the nineties of the last century). "The whole country has not had ten years' rest. The Ijaiye War of 1860 which extended to Iperu, Makun and Ikorodu and the

Eketiparapo and the Ibadan-Ilorin war are the offspring of this Opomu War. We are inclined to believe that the different tribes themselves cannot yet settle these differences, seeing that each tribe [1] has a hand in the causes which led to them."

Anyone wishing to know how this peace was accomplished by the British should read " Papers relative to the Reduction of Lagos," 1852, and "Correspondence respecting the War between native tribes in the Interior," 1887—two very interesting papers presented to both Houses of Parliament by command of Her late Majesty.

[1] This is interesting as at the present day many half-educated natives are apt to put down the ruin of their country to its occupation by British Government.

CHAPTER II

CREATION AND THE SACRED STONES AT IFE

Creation

THERE are many stories of creation among the Yoruba, but the story which I have chosen to open this study on the Genesis of the Yoruba is remarkable, I think, owing to the statement of Oja that the three parts representing God in Creation turned to stone when once they had set Creation going, leaving the carrying on of the work, it would appear, to sixteen great Orisha. Togun (see below) does not mention the word Olorun, the word now used to represent God, who is also known as Eleda the Creator, Elemi (the owner of breath). I think we shall learn as we proceed that he, as the owner of heaven, is a development of Jakuta, the father thunder god.

It was in the village of Ilobe in the Egbado district, S. Nigeria, that the following account of the Creation was given to me by an old lady called Oja who, the Bale or Chief told me, knew all about it. She was a Priestess, and spoke to me through a relation of hers called Togun, who was also connected with the Priesthood. Deputy Ranger Edwards acted as interpreter. Togun said, "In the beginning two people made the world, one Yemuhu and the man." "What man?" I asked. "Orishala, the husband of Yemuhu, who is also called Obaba Arugbo. When Yemuhu and Orishala came to the world they were afraid, and they were accompanied by Ajajuno, a person who was not made by anyone, and who acted as a messenger and war chief. She was a woman whose business it was to fight the world.

"When Yemuhu and Orishala had finished their work of Creation, and their visit to the world, they turned to stone—and when Orishala was about to turn to stone Yemuhu said she would also turn to stone *again*. But before they turned to stone Orishala had a ram tied to his waist by a rope, and Yemuhu had a gourd or calabash containing the sixteen snails,[1] and when she turned to stone these sixteen snails became the head of Eleda" (as we have noticed one of the names by which Olorun is said to be known).

"And what became of the ram?"

"I do not know."

"When Eleda arose he noticed that Ifa had no head.

"One day Eleda fighting with Ifa knocked him down, and his head came out, then his chest came out, then his nose, then his mouth and eyes. Orishala did this."

[1] These 16 snails are symbols of Odudua, another name evidently for Yemuhu.

CREATION AND SACRED STONES AT IFE

Here Togun paused, and the woman Oja gave him a small tin of palm oil. With this Togun oiled his tongue and then proceeded. "These stones are to be seen at Ife up to the present."

The Grove Sacred to Ore

On one of my tours through Yorubaland I went to Ife and stayed a day there (I should like to have stayed a year) and managed to hear a good deal of the departed changing into stones.

The Oni[1] of Ife was kind enough to send his clerk with me to show me over the "Grove Sacred to an old Oni of Ife called Ore."[2]

They say that to avoid a war this old Oni, his wife and son, retired to this grove and died, and were turned to stone. This grove is situated on the road about ten minutes outside the Eastern Gate of the city of Ife. Leaving the road and turning to the right we marched about 111 feet down a lane when we passed through a screen of palm leaves hanging from two Perigun trees. About ninety feet from this entrance on the left of the pathway we reached three stones, which they called Ogun; thirteen feet from here we passed through a kind of gateway which led us

STONES SACRED TO OGUN.

---

[1] Oni is the title of a chief who is much in the same position as the Archbishop of Canterbury is in England. It is also the name given to the firstborn.
[2] Ore means "Spirit of the departed." Not only did Orishala and Odudua turn to stone, but, as we shall learn, Ifa also.

20 NIGERIAN STUDIES [CHAP.

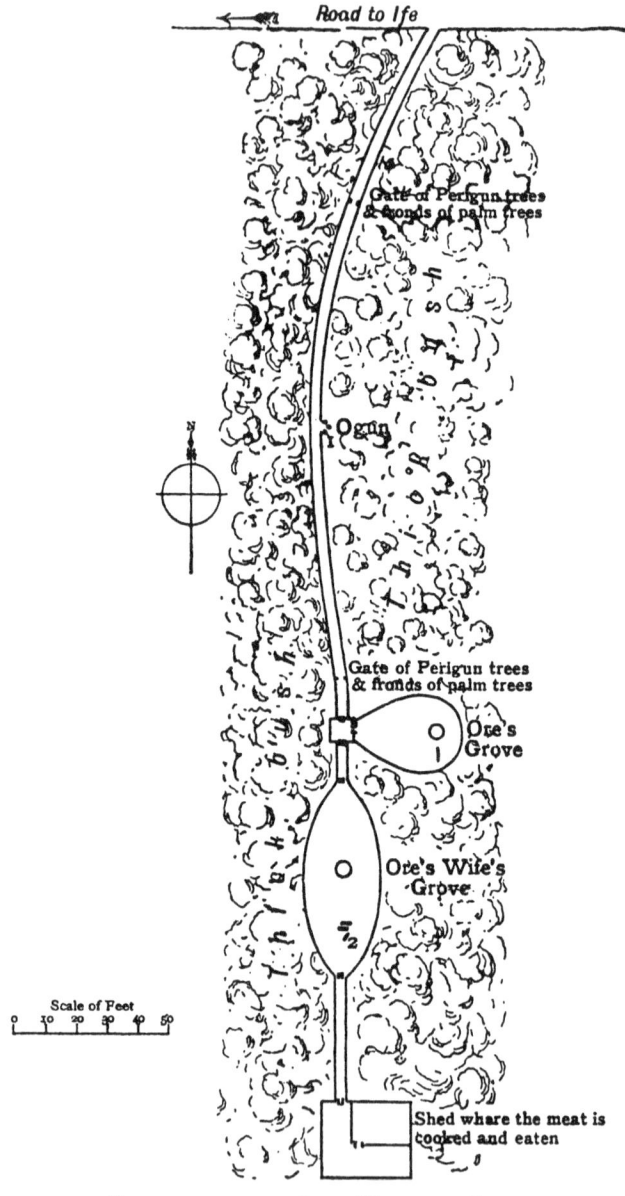

GROVES SACRED TO ORE, WIFE AND CHILD.

II CREATION AND SACRED STONES AT IFE

into a small square with two other gateways leading out of it, one to the East, and one to the South.

We first passed through the eastern gate and there under a small shed in the centre of the grove we saw the stone figure of Ore. He was only two feet eight inches in height, but three feet round the waist, so I came to the conclusion that this hero shrunk somewhat in height in the process of turning to stone. Near to him were two kola boxes or dishes in stone each one foot long and six inches wide. A stone which looked very much like a gravestone was standing to the south-east of the image. They said it had grown out of the ground. The width of this grove was about seventeen feet, and the length thirty-two feet.

IN ORE'S WIFE'S GROVE.

We went back to the porch and now passed through the entrance to the south which led us down a passage fifteen feet in length, and then we entered the enclosure, oval in shape and about sixty feet long, which was sacred to the wife of Ore.

About thirty-one feet from the entrance was a small circular shed under which the figure of Ore's wife stood. It measured three feet in height and two feet round the waist. Sixteen feet from this shed was a collection of interesting stones. Two were flat (one of which was broken) and measured four feet six inches by one foot and, three feet three inches by one foot respectively, and, rising from a mound of stones, a carved stone representing an elephant's tusk two feet six inches in height stood erect.

Passing out of this grove by a lane forty-three feet long we came to a clearing measuring twenty-three by twenty-eight feet near the side of which was a hut with mud walls, where, they said, the worshippers who had sacrificed to Ore came to cook and eat the flesh of the animals sacrificed. The clerk told me that this hut once contained a slab of rock upon which a crocodile was carved. We had a good look for it, but it was not there.

Other Sacred Stones at Ife

Morimi and Alashe, mother and son, having also turned to stones, are now worshipped as Orishas at Ife.

The Oni of Ife said that Alashe (the lawgiver) was Jesus,[1] the father of all white men, and he was not sure but he thought that he also was descended from him.

Alashe, he said, was the only child of Morimi who

[1] Did the Oni mean Moses?

STONE CHAIR PRESENTED TO SIR W. MACGREGOR BY THE ONI OF IFE, NOW IN THE BRITISH MUSEUM.

A CHAIR MARKET AT BADAGRY, S. NIGERIA.

II CREATION AND SACRED STONES AT IFE 23

was worshipped for having sacrificed her son to save the city from destruction. He pointed out the house she used to live in, which is quite near to his palace.

I also saw the house Alashe is said to have inhabited; it is situated down the hill to the east of the palace. In front of the house two poles had been placed in the ground and a sheet of white cloth was hanging from a string tied from pole to pole. Seven trees formed a kind of arbour in which were one or two sacred stones. Women dressed in white were kneeling here and there as if in prayer. Alashe's festival was then being held.

The story goes that when war was being waged against Ife, God threatened to destroy the city unless a woman with only one child, and that a male, was willing to sacrifice it. Now Morimi, who had only one child, Alashe, was a rich woman and did not wish to lose her wealth so she agreed to sacrifice her son.

When Alashe was about to be killed he and all his property were turned into stone. A chair or stool now in the British Museum was the property of Alashe. He had sent all his property to the palace of the Oni for safety while the war was on. The Oni said that when Captain Bower was pacifying the country he took the stool from Ife and gave it to Sir W. Macgregor, and he added, "when I went down to Lagos Sir William offered to give me the stool back but I refused to take it. I have another one left."

Quite close to the palace there are two large outcrops of quartz evidently similar to that from which these stools and other stone images were made, so we may conclude that they were made on the spot. But by whom? I am inclined to think that they must have been made by some black mason, possibly one of those natives sent to the King of Portugal in the fifteenth century and educated by the Portuguese, He may have returned as a lay brother or even as a priest and found his way to Ife. He then possibly introduced a form of Christianity and built two Churches, one dedicated to Jesus and one to the Virgin Mary. The stools were perhaps part of the furniture of these Churches.

OPA ORANYAN AT IFE.

But in Ife all sorts of people and things are turned to stone; the Oni has the figure in stone of a man caught in the act of having connection with his sister.

Just outside the town is the "stick" of Oranyan,[1] a

---

[1] Togun called the stone pillars, still to be seen in Ife, Orunmila, but the present Oni of Ife on my visit there called the pillar still standing Opa Oranyan, the stick or pole of Oranyan. Captain Elgee in his paper to the African Society translated the words as the walking stick of God,

rounded pillar eleven feet in height and three feet six inches in girth, with the remains of a second in two pieces by its side, also what may be the remains of a third. I asked the Oni if there had not been three pillars at one time and he gave me to understand that there had been, but that during the wars his enemies had taken one.

About a foot from the top of this pillar the present Alafin of Oyo on his visit to Ife had tied a piece of white cloth as a kind of act of submission, thereby putting on one side his religion as a Mohammedan. Near the centre of the pillar a horn and an axe are carved. Above these figures forty-five copper headed nails in three rows had been driven into the stone, on one side of it ten, and on the other eight, while below twenty of these curious nails still remain. I measured this stone with a tape and made it eleven feet in height. Captain Elgee makes it twelve, so that I can only conclude that we measured different sides of it.

I asked the Oni where the three sacred trees were,[1] but he hesitated to tell me. Then I told him about the three pillars of mud called Eshu and the three sacred trees at Iaiu. "Ah!" he said, " they got their religion from here."

Later on, while wandering about the town, I happened to descend from the plateau on which the Oni has his palace and march in an easterly direction. My attention was drawn to a woman who was standing before what seemed a heap of stones praying. As soon as she had gone I went into this grove and

[1] See Page 195 *At the Back of the Black Man's Mind.*

found two mounds of stones with the stumps of old trees in the centre and the remains of another heap of stones. This then was the place where the three Oyisa trees had once existed.

Opa Oranyan,[1] the stick or pole of Oranyan, is what the one standing pillar is called, and upon making enquiries I learnt that Opa is sometimes used as a slang word for penis. It is possible then that here in Ife, the cradle of the religion of the Yoruba people, as in Iaiu, the three pillars represented the three procreative persons, Father, Mother, Son, while the three trees (Oyisa)[2] figured the same three persons in their God.

Not far from the grove where I saw the woman addressing the three mounds of stone, and on the opposite side of the road, is an altar composed of stones sacred to the moon, called Oshupa Igio. Upon a large block of granite surrounded by some smaller blocks of the same substance are two slabs of granite on which rest two smaller stones about the size of one's fist. It is said that when the Babalawo rub the slabs with them they shine with a light like that of the moon. Amongst the stones alongside the altar were two pieces of cut quartz which evidently once represented the moon.

I should say that they were carved by the same artist who made the stools. Close to the altar were three smaller stones which they called Eshu (devil), and in a little clearing in the bush were two large pear-

---

[1] Called by Togun Orunmila.
[2] Bini for Orisha.

shaped stones which they called Orisha Omu, meaning breast, udder. Near to the palace of the Oni of Ife there is a well which is said to have no bottom, and they said this was not made by man but by the Orisha Olokorogbo.

CHAPTER III

DEATH, BURIAL, AND DEPARTED SPIRITS ORO EGUNGUN, ETC.

Egun.

IRO, Oro, Egun, Egungun, and Eleko, are all now Orishas representing the spirits of their ancestors, and it is during festivities connected with them that the "bull-roarer" appears. At Ilaro I noticed three trees with all their branches cut off[1] and the bark

[1] *Note by Adesola in the* Nigerian Chronicle.

The whole company of gods and men proceed outside to what is called the Oro pagi (Oro kills the tree) or Oro jegi (Oro eats the tree) ceremony. For its performance the newly deified takes the company to the highest tree in the neighbourhood in order to show proof of its divinity by "eating" up every leaf thereon to the latest shoot. At a convenient distance from this tree gods and men accommodate themselves as best as possible—the gods crying with all their might and the men drumming very loudly, singing and dancing at the same time. As it is not permitted to the uninitiated to know how this spirit feat is performed, suffice it to say that one wakes up in the morning to see that particular tree completely denuded of its leaves : and it will require the service of the most powerful microscope to discover even the tiniest and latest shoot anywhere about the tree up to the loftiest branch or on the surrounding surface or anywhere about the vicinity of the tree. These leaves are supposed to have been literally eaten up by the god. "A ki ri ajeku Oro" (No mortal ever sees the fragments of food devoured by the Oro god) has now passed into a by-word. Suspended on this tree between any two of its branches which are topmost, or sometimes left streaming on one of the branches which is the highest, is a new mat or a white or red piece of cloth. In rare but important cases the cloth is stretched from the branch of this particular

TREE PLANTED OVER GRAVE WHICH THUS BECOMES SACRED.

[*Face p.* 28.

CH. III DEATH, BURIAL, AND DEPARTED SPIRITS

round each stumped branch curled like a frill around it. On the top of each tree was a white flag. It was down these trees, I was told, that the spirit of the departed came to visit his relations. One of the chiefs of Ilaro had died some days before, and so, when I arrived there, people playing drums kept passing through the market on their way to the late chief's house. Just before dark, as the market people were assembling, an "Egun" presented himself before my tent, and told me that he was the father (deceased) come from heaven, and what was I going to give him. The men, they said, know that the Egun is a man

tree to that of another tree or trees in the same neighbourhood or at the nearest or furthest corner. You see it floating in mid-space high up in the air. What these mats or cloths are intended to symbolise ought to be evident from what I had pointed out in a previous article. [In the *Nigerian Chronicle*.] Unlike the *Egungun* (No. II) and Agemo (No. IV) the incarnated form of the *Oro* is never habited in cloths and mats. What its nature and habiliments are is supposed to be a mystery and jealously guarded up to the present from the gaze of women. In fact *Oro* is worshipped more in its inane and spiritual form than in a materialised shape. It is to the former that sacrifices are offered, not to the latter. Among the Egbas who are the originators of this cult, the *Oro awe* ceremony is the only funeral rite performed in connection with this worship when the spirit is supposed to pass from the "unburied" (No. III) into the "buried" state. Viewing it in this connection the mat or cloths suspended on the tree must be taken to represent the mats or cloth with which the dead was buried; and its suspension to signify that the spirit of the deceased now purified with funeral rites and having entered into that stage of spirit life in which it can be invoked and worshipped, casts behind it in its flight into the spirit world these earthly encumbrances as being useless to it.

After the completion of this Oro-pagi ceremony they (gods and men) again repair to the house; and having regaled themselves with the remnants, they re-form into a procession, remove the *mariwo* from the gate, march direct for the *Abore's* and thence to their own house ere break of day. In the morning the inmates return to the houses of mourning, set a mark to the dedicated spot, and congratulate one another that the departed had passed into the *Oro* stage and can be invoked at any time for worship.

dressed up, but they respect the dress and keep up the play for the sake of the women-folk whom, they say, need this assurance (that the chief has risen from the dead). This Egun wore top boots made by the Hausa. He also wore pants instead of the native cloth. His shirt and overcloth were of a rich texture, but not different from that worn by the well-to-do. But he wore a net-like mask in front of his face which gave him a weird appearance. Men and boys followed him, and seemed to be much impressed when the Egun cried out in a voice evidently not his own : " I am from heaven, therefore you must respect me."

When an important man dies in these parts, his relations wash his body, and then shave off all hair. Then they smear the body over with redwood and water. The body is now placed on a mat on the ground. The two big toes are tied together, and the hands are placed on the chest. The mouth and nostrils are filled with cotton wool. Each of the children of the deceased then brings a fine cloth and covers the body. Then they call all the people, who come and condole with them. If the deceased's daughter has a little one, it is this grandchild who sits near to the deceased's bed and fans him. During the night they have four or five lights burning. People from all around come playing the gong-gong drums. They remain all night and are given food and drink by the children of the deceased. Among the rich this feasting is kept up for seven days before the body is buried. If the deceased has left a married daughter, it is her husband who digs the grave. He gets ten or twenty men to help him, and pays them in goods. On the evening before the burial the son and daughter give money to buy a sheep or goat. Then they take the corpse to the grave, and having placed the body in it the goat or sheep is killed over it, so that the blood falls upon it. The sons and daughters must next weep so that their tears may also fall on the corpse. The grave is then filled in.

Regarding these expenses Adesola writes :

> "Otalelegbeje ro gba
> Omo re a san ligbehin o
>
> The amount you have received
> Will some day be paid by your children.

"[Otalegbeje is 1460 cowries, or 36 strings and a half. It is not intended to be interpreted literally. One of the many things which contribute to the heaviness of funeral expenses in Yorubaland is the amount that must be paid the various social, religious and political guilds to which the deceased is attached, apart from presents of yams, oil, goats, and other cattle and provisions which must be made at some definite time after interment or during the celebration of the funeral ceremonies. The amount is for making etutu (propitiatory sacrifices) for the dead; the provisions to maintain the members when they meet. There is no native but belongs to one or another of these guilds. Some belong to several and a man's rank is estimated according to the guild or guilds to which he belongs. Whatever amount remains after the necessary expenses are made is distributed among the members and every individual is given a portion, however small, in proportion to his official status. The enjoyment of this benefit is regarded as an accumulated debt for every individual and imposes an obligation upon their children to make similar contribution to the guild towards their parents' funerals at their deaths. This song repeated at funerals is to keep them always in recollection of this fact. This expense is always heaviest in connection with the Ogboni (Senatorial) Society. This is both a political, social and a secret Society. In fact it is the King's chief consultative chamber in all matters and its principal members form the Cabinet. They lay the corpse with full masonic rites. In their passage to and from the house of mourning, they sound alarms with their state drums of various height and sounds so that every woman or uninitiated man might flee their presence either in the street or in the house of mourning. For a woman to see them or their drum (in the old days) meant death ; for an uninitiated man a very heavy fine with compulsory initiation. During the process of corpse-laying they continue beating their drums and so at intervals whilst the corpse is still lying in state when they go to make their etutu. At each time they are generally provided with palm wine and native beer. The members are sometimes called Oshugbo. A few elderly women are always admitted and these are generally distinguished from others by having certain cotton strings (okun) tied round their wrists : such women are supposed to be for ever precluded from marriage. Members of this Society sometimes professed Christianity in order to free their children from the above obligation.]"

MEMBERS OF A FUNERAL SECRET SOCIETY IN LAGOS CALLED ADAMORISHA, WEARING DRESSES SIMILAR TO THE EGUNGUN, EGUN.

"PORO" HOUSE.

[*Face p.* 32.

They present all who condole with them with kola, gin, rum, or palm wine. In the olden days, if they had not the money, they would rather sell themselves to be able to stand the expense than not entertain in a fitting manner. They would work one week for their owner, and one week for themselves until they had saved sufficient to redeem themselves.

To prove to the women folk that man rises and goes to heaven a person is placed in a private room. Then when all the family is assembled in an adjoining room someone will strike the ground three times with a stick crying out, " Father ! Father! Father ! Answer me." And the Egun, the person in the room, answers and every one rejoices. Food has been placed in the Egun's room by the women, and when the Egun has answered each guest goes in there and helps himself as he or she likes. The Egun is not dressed up when in this room, but if he wishes to go outside and join in the dancing then he dresses himself and puts on his mask.

Oro or the Bull Roarer.

Colonel Ellis (p. 3, *The Yoruba-speaking Peoples*) writes, " Just as Egungun is now used for social purposes, and to preserve order in private life, so is Oro used for political purposes, to preserve order in the community at large ; yet, from the analogy of other peoples, and from the fact that it is death for a woman to see the instrument which produces the voice of Oro, there can be no doubt that Oro was the spirit that presided at the celebration of male mysteries, such as are found among the Kurnai of Australia, and he has perhaps been diverted from his proper purpose by the influence of the Ogboni."

A story which rather bears out the phallic origin of Oro is as follows :—

Another name for Oro is Iro, a chimpanzee or slave of a rich man. His master had no child, and so, when he bought Oro, he asked him what work he could do. Oro said that the only work he knew how to do was to offer sacrifice to the Orishas. And promised his master that if he would allow him to do this kind of work only he would see that he got a child. Then Oro went to search for camwood and made two flat pins. In these he made holes at the end and tied strings to them. And anyone who heard the sound when he whizzed them through the air had children. Then his master had children also and asked Oro what he would take for the good work he had done for him. He asked for a ram and pito[1] and that is why the Oro cries, " Mu de lewe, lewe, lewe, lewe " ("I come with young, young, young"). And now his worshippers sacrifice ram, dog, and pito, and never eat dog and horse. And he who offends him brings a dog as an offering. But his followers will not eat it. When his master had some children Oro killed one and ate it. Then the master asked him : " Why did you kill my child and eat it ? " Then Oro ran away and lived in

[1] Corn beer.

III DEATH, BURIAL AND DEPARTED SPIRITS 35

the forests and became a chimpanzee,[1] and from that time he was called IRO OMO NENUN the chimpanzee, the child of Nenun.

And now if anyone wants a child from Oro he will get a ram and pito and take it to the forests and call him three times " O-o-oro, O-o-oro, O-o-oro." The third time he answers, " Mu de lewe, lewe, lewe."

All the people went to Nenun and asked him where his slave "Oro" had gone? He said to the bush. He did his best to get him to come back but he would not. So when men want a

[1] *Nigerian Chronicle.*

ADESOLA'S VERSION OF THE IRO STORY.

"An ape (Iro) who had the power of transforming itself into a human being made love during one of his transformations with a woman who was in the habit of collecting jungle products for the market. Several children (boys) were the result of this amorous affection. Their rendezvous was a retreat in the woods where the ape who often came in the guise of a hunter signalled his approach and arrival by means of what now becomes the *Oro* spirit cry. For the amusement of his children and to give them a dance, he beat his breast for a drum. The sound of it was what is now imitated by the *Obete and Asipelu* drums used whenever an Oro function takes place. He greatly enriched both wife and children by means of the product of the chase, the latter of whom also embraced his profession. He ultimately retained his human form and at his death was buried on the spot which was their meeting place. Having shown himself a very extraordinary personage during his lifetime, he was worshipped as a god after his death ; and whenever his children would invoke his *manes* they produce the same sound by the same means and beat the same drums as their father was in the habit of producing and beating."

This story evidently is an invention with a purpose. It is to explain the *Oro* as a deified spirit ; only it makes it the deified spirit of one individual rather than of many. The tradition of the man ape is to give it (the Oro) a divine origin ; for apes and other species of that genus are sacred animals in the Yoruba country. Parents of twins and people who worship *Ibeje* (the twin gods) will never kill or eat monkeys, as twins are supposed to be the transformations of these creatures that often displace the foetus of children. The derivation of *Oro* from *Iro* as explained by the above tradition cannot therefore hold.

child now they first bring the ram and pito to the Oro grave,[1] and ask Nenun to take the offering to Oro. The reason why women may not see Iro is that having killed the child, they told the mother that the child was lost and so deceived her but they took Oro's clothes from him so that he was naked, and ashamed to see women.

Women run away because his master has punished Oro by not allowing him to wear clothes and return to town. It is not Oro but only his symbol that comes to town.

The flat piece of camwood is called ISHE and

---

[1] *Nigerian Chronicle*, September 10th, 1909.
BURIAL CUSTOMS IN THE YORUBA COUNTRY BY ADESOLA

Oro's grove is a *sanctum sanctorum* and no one, whatever be his rank or status dare enter it unless he is a devotee and that on special and rather rare occasions. As a matter of fact it brooks no interference; and wherever and whenever an *Oro* cry is heard no *Egungun* or *Eluku* dare cry there at the same time. It is regarded as the chief of the spirit gods and it maintains its awe and dignity intact even under modern conditions. Apart from the rites and ceremonies performed in the grove, there are other demonstrations performed in the public; but from all, whether done within the grove or without it, women are rigidly excluded. All males from the baby at the back to the centenarian have access to the witnessing of its public demonstrations. I have made independent inquiries from several people who are Egba-born whether that special privilege, that is extended to some elderly women, called *Iya Agan*, of initiation into the Egungun mysteries is ever granted to any woman in the *Oro* mysteries and in each instance have received a negative reply. One gentleman alone it was who told me this privilege was conceded to his late grandmother but I have every reason to doubt his veracity. It was reported of that wealthy Egba woman who gave a name to one of our public Squares in Lagos with some of its buildings that on her return to her native country she offered to buy the exceptional privilege of being initiated into the mysteries of this spirit god and of gaining its acquaintance, To this end she used all the influence her great wealth gave her, but she had to spend an equal if not a greater amount to recant and that within doors and on her knees when the god and his attendants came in front of her compound to accept the invitation.

III DEATH, BURIAL AND DEPARTED SPIRITS

the string is called AsHo Oro or Oro's Cloth. The stick to which the string is tied is called Papa Oro, Oro's stick.

Another form is the Agbe which is a piece of flat wood about two feet long attached to a string tied to a ball of cloth, grass, or string called Ibowo Oro, Oro's handle.

Ishe represents a young man, but Agbe a full grown man.

Ishe is that which makes. Agbe is that which lives. And my informant told me that they were symbols of the Phallus.

Oro is a man's Orisha, and all men should worship him.

He was the first man slave bought from God by Nenun, therefore men should recognise and worship him, as the giver of children.

When a person dies the relations cry out, "Oro o Baba o," because Oro was the first Orisha and first father who caused men to have children. To refer to the living father is not solemn enough; the death cry refers to their first father Oro.

The calling of Oro by the Ogbonis is only to frighten women away, as they do not wish them to see how they execute a criminal.

Mr. Pellegrin told me that when the first yams are ready the Egba worshipped Oro. No woman enters the Oro bush, and if he comes out night or day the women must go indoors. A ram is killed and cooked, and its head is placed on the wall near to the worshipper's father's grave.

They draw a figure of a man in white chalk on the wall near the grave, to represent the departed. It is on this figure that they hang the head of the ram. And a stranger will know if the head has not been replaced each year.

They used to appoint a man called OLOGBO IJEUN, the chief of the Oro ceremony, who noted the seasons and appointed the time for the beginning of Oro ceremony,

In the "Head Hunters" Dr. Haddon gives a description of the Malu ceremonies,[1] and I am sure that any of us who have seen Oro will be quite ready to recognise the masked Zogole as some very near relation.

This Malu ceremony, however, has to do with the initiation of youths to certain male mysteries, while our Oro, as figured by the bull roarer, is said not only to be the giver of children, but to arrest disease and sickness, and prevent so many people dying. In this it more nearly represents the "Maduh" (p. 107) that used to "turn devil" at night time, and go round the the gardens, and swing bull roarers to make the yams grow. Or perhaps Uvio is still more like our Oro, for "if anyone is sick, food is given to Uvio, who is placed on the top of a big house (clarino) and he is addressed 'Oh! Uvio, finish the sickness of our dear one, and give life.'"

It is strange that the Yoruba do not connect "Oro" with the male mysteries, when it is so openly

[1] Vols. V. and VI. *Reports of Cambridge Expedition to Torres Straits.*

a male ceremony, but of many people I have asked some say they have never heard of Oro in this connection, and others will not hear of any such thing being mentioned. I say strange,[1] because the bull roarer is certainly used at Ovia's yearly festival in Benin territory, at which as certainly youths are initiated into the male mysteries. It is also used in the worship of Ovato at Geduma, and during the Ebomici festival and Ihoho dance at Ugo, both also in the Benin Kingdom, which, as you may be aware, is a Kingdom adjoining the Yoruba conntry and said to have been founded by a son of a Yoruba Oni of Ife. But it may be that while "Oro" is present on these occasions it is only as a deterrent to women and others not to pry into the secrets of the Orisha, or so-called Deity.

At Igbore the Oro festival is held always about September, and it is at this time that members are initiated into the secrets of the fraternity. Certain youths known to be capable of keeping secrets are chosen as novices.

The Oro of the Bini is known as Oloawon Ovato Oloawon Ovia, and Usaokwhaiyi, that is the Oloawon in connection with the Orishas Ovato, Ovia and Okwhaiyi.

Oloawon means the owner of the turtle or tortoise,[2] the essence of deceit and meanness. He is described as one who is constantly deceiving men and other animals, and leading them to their death by making

---
[1] See *At the Back of the Black Man's Mind*, page 211.
[2] The turtle is called the sea-tortoise.

use of secrets with which he has been entrusted. He leads women also to seduction and other crimes.

To prove that boys are not like women and the tortoise, such as are chosen as novices to be initiated into the secrets of the fraternity of Ovia or Ovata are first given a supposed secret to keep. After a time if it is found that the boys have not told even their mothers anything about it, they are tried again and again, seven times in all, when, if considered trustworthy, they are taken to the Orisha's grove at the beginning of the yearly festival, and gradually taught the secrets of the craft. The Festival of Ovia continues for some three months, and at the end of this time Oloawon (or Oro) comes down for seven days, and Ovia is then said to be dead until next year. During these seven days women are not allowed outside their houses.

Anyone at other times of the year is allowed to enter the grove or temple of Ovia, and to ask its help to destroy his or her enemies. If the enemy has done something worthy of death, Ovia gives him a certain medicine in the making up of which parts of the tortoise or turtle are used.[1] The criminal is said to swell up and die.

It is interesting in this connection to read in the *Head Hunters* (page 106): "Before going out *turtling* the men marched round the Agu and whirled the 'bull roarers' alway circling clockwise."

When a great man dies the "Ogboni"[2] go and

[1] Vol. V. of *Cambridge Expedition to Torres Straits.*
[2] Native council.

lay him out and help to bury him. On their way they cry out 'Ehpa Ogboni Enu! Enu!" translated to me as :—The Ogboni are coming, catch him! catch him! (referring to anyone they may find outside their houses). When they have buried the defunct Oro comes.

When the "Ogboni" are holding a palaver or trying a case they beat certain tunes on a drum; if they condemn the person to death, the tune beaten on the drum is changed to Oro [1] and all the people know of

---

[1] *Nigerian Chronicle*, 17th September.
BURIAL CUSTOMS IN THE YORUBA COUNTRY.
Oro or Spirit-Worship among the Egbas.
By ADESOLA.
The political aspect of Oro Worship.

Oro worship has a political side. The god assisted the State to give capital punishment to criminals in return for services rendered it by the state. As with punishment meted out by its companion gods, social disgrace follows because of its implications. The Oro decapitates (*pa*) in which case the head of the criminal is nailed to a tree as a warning to others; or takes away (*gbe*) the criminal, body and soul, out of the arena of life when neither the living man nor the lifeless is ever seen after. To the shades of such criminals no funeral honours are given, no shrines erected, no worship paid. Their spirits are supposed to be doomed to roam eternally outside the spirit world. With the *Oro* they revisit the earth on festive occasions only to wander about in corner places. Hence they are called *Pakoko* (loiterers in the corner). They are often referred to as *Eru Oro* (Oro slaves). For these reasons an *Egba* man would quickly resent the imprecation *Oro re ma gbe e* or *Oro re ma pa e* (May you fall a prey to the Oro god).

The *Oro* is also employed as an instrument of banishment. If the state considers it expedient to expel anyone from the country and the authorities find themselves powerless to accomplish the object, they concede the business to the *Oro* god. As soon as ready, an *Oro* confinement is, declared, *i.e.* every woman is to keep within doors. The gods then begin to walk the streets (Oro gbode). As many of them surround the house of the individual giving out their weird cries; and eventually the man is heard miles off away from the town. He is then said to be banished by the *Oro* (*won fi Oro le nilu*).

In times of great political crisis or whenever the state would undertake

their decision. When some of the "Ogboni" belong to the Oro fraternity they can call "Oro" out and there is no doubt that at times they have abused this privilege.

After witnessing the Egungun ceremony already described, a semi-educated native, who evidently thought he had got me in a favourable position to annoy, volunteered the statement that the Government for some reason or other would not allow Oro to kill inquisitive women he found out of doors and that in consequence they were getting quite out of hand. What were they to do? I looked at that semi-educated barbarian who had certainly been sufficiently in touch with civilisation to know exactly why the Government put down this class of murder, and suggested that he should write to the "Society for the Protection of Aborigines." (This class of native has got to look upon this Society as something a little more powerful than the Secretary of State for the Colonies and the Government he represents, and appeals to it in some cases after appealing to the Secretary of State to redress some fancied grievance.)

Mr. Pellegrin remembers how on one occasion Oro was called "accidentally" at Abeokuta when three men

the consideration of any new law or measure that will seriously affect the several sections of the country, an *Oro* confinement is also declared. The streets being thus cleared of traffic and women save such as are carried on under the circumstances by the men, the several heads and sub-heads of the various townships often travel to attend conference. Any decision arrived at in this assembly becomes law and is considered binding on the whole country. Confinements are again declared whenever a state sacrifice is to be offered on behalf of the town. In this instance the gods parade the streets and the dull monotony which would have prevailed is relieved by singing, dancing and other *Oro* displays.

were to be executed. Jaguna the executioner killed the first, killed the second and when he got to the third, who was the youngest of them, his cutlass would not cut. He tried it three times without success, so he went back to his seat and got a revolver and shot him in the head. The young man cried out and put his hand to his head and took the bullet and said, "Jaguna, here is your bullet." Jaguna then fired into the young man's ear. He shook his head and the bullet dropped out of his other ear into his hand. He gave the bullet to Jaguna. Then the people cried out Oro and the women ran away. Then the people hacked the criminal to pieces with their knives. These criminals had been condemned to death for selling salt to the Ibadan, then the enemies of the Egbas.

Asani, who says he remembers the tragedy, declares that three days afterwards the third culprit was seen by him in the town, and that his people begged him to go away as it was against the law of Oro for a man who had been killed by Oro to come to life again.

A man who will not be killed and lives in spite of being executed in this way is called Ologun or a medicine man. Alateshe, an Egba Chief, refused to allow a man who had been thus executed to be killed again, as he said some day this rascality would save them.

When the Egba go to war and set the Ishe (Oro) whizzing and the enemy hears it he runs away.

Anyone who is an Oro worshipper must attend the funeral of a member of the craft. The one who is burying the worshipper gives the Oro, a ram, pito, and kola. With the kola they touch the dead man's head. Then with their fists closed, thumbs inside and one hand on the other, they touch the dead man's head three times and then the head of his son who is succeeding him. They next take the kola again and touch the dead man's head three times and then the child's head, asking the dead to bless the living. Then they kill the ram, and the children of the deceased rub their foreheads with the blood. This sacrifice is repeated every year by the children, and they tie the head of the ram on the wall near to the grave (in the house).

Talking of the persecution of the early Christians Miss Tucker, in her book *Abeokuta*, writes: "Idinui . . . died in the Ake Mission house. His master (Mr. Hinderer) obtained the consent of his relatives and buried him in the Christian burying ground . . . It was the first case of the death of a native convert; and the Ogboni who have by law, it appeared, the arrangement and the profits of all the funerals, considered their right was infringed upon and lost no time in taking advantage of the alleged misdemeanour. Six of the converts were seized and confined in the Council House of Itoku . . . Mr. Hinderer . . . procured their release after five days of suffering, not however without severe scourging.

" The Missionaries received intelligence from the Obashorun . . . who was unvarying in the friendliness of his conduct towards them, that the Chief of Igbore was intending to follow the example of Itoku."

"Nothing," writes Mr., afterwards Bishop, Crowther, "was omitted that could make the circumstances appalling to the poor sufferers; Oro was called out . . . the Ogboni drums were beating furiously and a great multitude armed with bill hooks, clubs and whips were catching and dragging our poor converts to the Council House . . . The women were cruelly scourged and pinioned without regard to age or sickness; and while all this was going on in the Council House, the houses of the imprisoned were being plundered, their household utensils destroyed, their doors unhinged and carried away."

Page 148.—"The fear of man kept back another person from becoming a candidate."

"It was a Priestess who had formerly been a violent opponent . . . . She feared lest if it were known she had embraced the new Religion she should in revenge be given to Oro, or in other words be murdered."

"This mysterious power Oro is an object of the greatest dread to the women of Abeokuta, who are forbidden to appear in the street during any of his visits under pain of death." (Ibid., page 173.)

The above was written in 1853. The Rev. R. H. Stone somewhere about the year 1860 (there is no date in his book, "In Africa's Forest and Jungle," neither has the publisher given the date of publication) says: "During my ten years' residence in Abeokuta the town was frequently given to Oro and on three occasions malefactors were punished and political matters of importance were transacted. The Voice of Oro was frequently heard in the streets after dark. It began in a low moan, then rose to a kind of scream and then sank into a moan. This noise was made by the whirling of a flat stick, but it was a capital crime for anyone to imitate as much.[1] It was a capital crime, also, for any woman to remain in the streets after the voice of Oro was heard at any time.

My friend, Mr. John Parkinson, collected two versions of the origin of Oro, which I have also heard, but take the liberty of giving in his own words. (See "*Man*," 1906, 66.)

The Legend of Oro.[2]

By John Parkinson.

In the olden days Olorun made six people, four men and two women, to whom after a certain time children were born, but these children always died.

And the people said to Olorun, "O Olorun, how is this; you made six people, and although children are born, they never live?" So they said, "We will find out another god who will let the children live."

Now amongst the four men, two were Babalawo (a priesthood who used the palm nut as a means of divination).

Then said the Babalawo, "Olorun is your father, but you must have some 'idol'[3] to worship

---

[1] Small boys now use it as a toy, 1909.
[2] Oro, the bull-roarer. See Ellis, *The Yoruba-speaking People of the Slave Coast of West Africa*, 109.
[3] "Idol," used in the sense of a visible and tangible object of veneration.

too." The others replied, "We are ready, let us know the name of this god"; and the Babalawo replied, "It is Oro, you must worship him."

So the Babalawo made the Oro, and brought it to the others and said, "You must give food every day." They answered, "That is good, but how shall we make him talk if we want anything of him?" To this the Babalawo replied that when the food was given the people should dance, and sing and clap their hands. And so doing, the Oro began to talk, saying,[1] "Baba ma mu-o" ("O father don't take them").[2] Since the people did this none of their children died, but the women were hidden in the house. Slowly the numbers of the people increased, and after a time they thought they would like to have a king, and they made a king. The king said, "I will worship only Oro, the god that makes us populous."

When the time for the yearly feast was come, the king gave a bullock to be killed, and he said, "I am king, and I do like a king. All my wives are to be present when Oro sings." And the wives were brought, and the bullock was killed, and the people danced and sang.

Then the king said, "I am king; how is it that common wood can talk and say [3] 'Baba ma mu-o'?"

But when Oro saw that women were present he

---

[1] Approximately onomatopoetic of the sound made by the "Bull-roarer."

[2] The pronoun them is not expressed in the original.

[3] "A woman was once splitting fire-wood in the streets. Accidentally a chip of it flew up and made a sound; she took up the piece and shewed it to the husband, he took it from her, contrived the Ise or Abe after it and ingeniously evolved the Oro worship.

kept silence. Then said the two Babalawo, "It is against the rules that women should be present when Oro is made, but since you are king we could not dictate to you at first, but now you yourself have proved that this cannot be done, for Oro does not cry where women are. This is not simply wood but Eru Male, the slave of Male (Male = Oro)."

And the king said to his wives, "Go home," and they went; and the Babalawo said, "Sing again."

Then as once more they sang, the Oro cried, "Baba ma mu-o." Hence it is from that day Oro is not made in the presence of women.

A Second Legend of Oro. In the earliest time six men were made by God, and the place where they lived was called Aking-oro (full of Oro). In those days this place was surrounded by bush and trees, and now and again the people could hear a sound, or cry, of "Mamu, ma mu," and so afraid were they that they dared not go into the forest. On a certain day one of them said, "I had a dream, and in the dream Olorun said, 'You must go from this place because it is Aking-oro, full of Oro.'"

But they answered, "We will not go from here; we will find animals and kill them as a sacrifice, sprinkling blood upon the ground to appease Oro." This ceremony they carried out, but the dreams came again, and, worst of all, their children died.

Now in those days Oro was a hunter, and Oro came into their country. When the people saw this hunter they were surprised and said, "Where do you come from; we thought there were but six of us?" Then Oro replied, "I came to tell you that this place belongs to me, and I will show you a spot where you can see me always," and he showed it to them and they cleared it. He told them that when they wanted to perform the ceremony of sacrifice to appease the spirit calling "Ma mu, ma mu," they should sing, and he would come and see them in the spot they had cleared. Moreover, Oro said, "When this spot is cleared, come every seven days and bring fowls, and sheep, and Fufu"[1] (fufu is mashed yam), and they went on the days indicated and Oro came as he had said.

When Oro had done eating he said, "I will make you a present." Then said one, "May I ask you something? You are the owner of this place, and since we have been here we hear the sound of 'Ma mu, ma mu.' What is this noise, since you are the owner of the place?"

And Oro replied, "I am the man who makes that noise every night." Then he cut a piece out of his forearm and gave it to them. But they said, "What shall we do with it?" Oro replied, "I am very old and cannot always come here every seven days, but when you come, bore a hole in the flesh and place a thread in it, and when you fling it outwards it will cry like me, being part of me. Take care, moreover, that no woman comes, and when you have finished with the piece of flesh put it in the ground before going home. You dare not take it to the house. And you will call this place Ebu Male" (Ebu = bush, Male = a name for Oro).

[1] Fufu is not a Yoruba word, mashed yam is called "Iyan."

Then they worshipped Oro every seven days, and the children ceased from dying, and the people multiplied.

When they became populous they elected a king.

Now the king had a wife whom he greatly loved, and the wife said, " I know you love me very much and I have a favour to ask of you. It is this: May I see the thing that cries at night?" And the king said, " It is against the rules, but I will let you see it, for I love you greatly."

So when the day for the feast came the king had a big chair made with a seat inside for the woman.

Arrived at the place they made the usual feast, and, as before, took the flesh from the ground and flung it out, but there came no sound. Then one of the four elders said, " Something is wrong here; the hunter said, ' No woman must come,' or he would fail to answer. We have called upon Ita (Oro) but there has been no answer, let us look at the king's chair." Then one went to the king's chair and broke it and saw the king's wife inside, and they began again to fling the flesh of the hunter into the air when suddenly the thread broke and the flesh flew off and cut the throat of the woman.

Then said the small piece of flesh, " I go to my father and will tell him what I have seen here to-day, but since you have broken the rule I must change myself, and on the next feast-day you will see what I have taken to fill my place.

When all had gone the piece of flesh told the hunter what had happened, and Oro the hunter came back, and Oro said, " Come to my flesh again," and Oro cut a stick and tied a string to it and left it in the ground.

Then Oro departed from the world, being offended because a woman had seen part of him.

Note the legend adds that Oro went into the cam-wood, hence any "Oro" made from cam-wood is held to be especially good. These stories of Oro, the bull-roarer, do not seem to be opposed to Ellis's suggestion that Oro was originally the spirit presiding at male mysteries, but my carriers do not know, or do not admit this idea.[1]

JOHN PARKINSON

---

[1] *Nigerian Chronicle, September 3rd. by Niepos ara Orun.*

In regard to derivation the word Oro is a purely onomatopoetic one and is derived from the sound heard at the discovery of the Abe or Ise of the musical God.

With respect to the origin. Although I am neither a missionary nor a parson, but only a grandson of Oro worshippers, I am almost ashamed to narrate the circumstance which led to the apotheosis of the God of my fathers. On a certain day in Orun ("Sun"), a town in the Egba Province of Gbagura, situated about 8 miles from Ibadan and lying on the route between Ijebu and Ibadan, as a certain woman was splitting wood for culinary purposes, there flew *from the clefts of the wood* something which made a whizzing sound similar to the "voice" of the God Oro. The astonished woman looked round and picked up that whizzing something which corresponded in shape with the Ise or Abe now employed in the worship of the god. Her husband being hard by, she shewed him the whizzing material and said in the dialect of "Orun" *Ese ti o ro baun* ("*why did it sound like that?*") *and the husband answered O ro be nani* ("*it simply sounded like that*") or something to the effect which led to the coining of the word Oro. The wily husband took the material from her and ere long invented the Ise or Abe, and with the aid of his companions the mystifying Oro worship was soon evolved. The old town of Orun is now called Podo or Oke orun, and is like Ibadan and a few other towns at the present time chiefly inhabited by Oyo people after it had been evacuated by the Egba as a result of the Owu war (1821-1830) which caused the dispersal of the Egba people and the destruction of the Egba towns.

As a proof of the truth of this story of the Origin of Oro custom it may be stated here that in the township of Orun in Abeokuta where the remnant of the people of old Orun now dwells since the founding of Abeo-

In each account it says that six beings were made by God. We shall note as we proceed how this number six keeps recurring as the number of the pairs of members of the council of different Societies.

Oro means, I am told, "lamentation," such as we now hear at funerals; as soon as the "father" dies, the family cry out *Epa! Oro o! Baba Lo, l'oni o.* Alas the departed one, the father has gone to-day!

In the second version Oro comes to the six as a spirit of the departed (Ore) or as Oro is now said to come.

In this version Oro cuts a piece out of his forearm, but I heard that it was another part of his anatomy (and I must here add that the time has not yet come for the people of this country to be quite frank in these matters, the followers of Oro are still very powerful and will punish the divulging of secrets of this sort, if they can).

I would draw your attention to page 65, "Great Benin," where Mr. C. Punch is made to say, "With these parts of the slain men and women the Oba is said to have made certain medicine for fetish purposes."

Although I have not been able to procure a leather "bull-roarer" it is well to remember that in the first version Oro is made to say, "this is not simply wood," and in the second, "when you have finished

kuta in 1830 to this day it is a woman that "Heralds the Oro" (Lo Oro) at the annual Oro festival which takes place in this township about Easter time each year.

with the piece of flesh" and "then said the small piece of flesh."

Certain parts of the dead Father are preserved by the Bakutu. The penis is cut off and smoked and then worn as a charm by his first wife's eldest son.

"Come to my flesh again," says Oro, and he cut a stick and tied a string to it and left it in the ground. Then Oro departed from the world, being offended because a woman had seen part of him.

Another reason given to me for the exclusion of women from affairs of state apart from their inability to keep a secret, was that wherever a man was, a woman came from here and another from there and both wished to become his friend (lover) and hence quarrels and fights ensued, and that men had formed this fraternity of "Oro" out of self-protection.

The following uses of the word Oro given by Mr. Adesola in *The Nigerian Chronicle*, September 24, 1909, appear to me to be most interesting:—

"The important place assigned to the worship of this god by the Egbas and other Yoruba tribes who have adopted it, the strictest privacy with which its rites and ceremonies are observed and the unflinching severity with which it punishes criminals give rise to an extended use of the term *Oro* to denote (1) any god, especially those with whose worship private rites and ceremonies are associated; (2) any secret society; (3) any secret rite or ceremony; (4) any strong or wicked man; (5) any very severe punishment; (6) any unpleasant and habitual characteristics of a man,

(7) an expression of great surprise. The following are illustrative sentences of the above.

(1) Egungun l'oro ilu wa ati ti idile wa.
Egungun is our national and household god.

(2) Awon ol'oro li eyi.
These are the members of a secret or friendly society.

(3) A mi s'oro loni No III.
We are performing the rites to-day. No III.

(4) Oro nini
That's he, a very wicked man (lit. He is an Oro indeed).

Oko yi ti m'oro.
You have not known the tyrant (lit. the Oro).

Oro agbolu aje.
A strong man that can dare anything (the expression literally is :—*Oro* that can remove from the arena of life the chief of the craft of witches. Any woman termed the head-witch is always supposed to be inaccessible to punishment even by the state; the business is often entrusted to the *Oro*).

(5) Kini se omode ni ti nke? Iya re nsoro fun ni.
Why is that child crying? The mother is giving him a severe punishment (lit. doing Oro for him).

Okonrin na mbo. Jowo re ma soro fun u.
The man is approaching you. Leave him. I'll teach a lesson (lit. I'll make the Oro for him).

Wa ki nforo han o.
Come near and let me teach you a lesson (lit. show you Oro).

(6) Omode na puro ju. Oro re ni ati ti idile won.
That boy tells awful lies. It is characteristic of him and his people (lit. it is the Oro worshipped by him, &c. A man's disposition is here regarded as the moral god to which he bows).

(7) Oro o! or Oro Baba o!
"By Jove" (lit. Thou Oro of my father. This cry is heard all about the streets from men and boys whenever the Oro gods are out; and it is that by which the spirit is invoked. Although the spirits of females are supposed to enter into the deified state yet the Oro spirits of males alone are invoked and worshipped. Really the Oro is regarded as the deified spirits of males. This is so because men only take part in its rites and ceremonies).

DEATH, BURIAL AND DEPARTED SPIRITS

In the Burial customs in the Yoruba country Mr. Adesola gives a most interesting account of the annual worship of "Eluku"[1] the Oro of the Ijebu, to which I must refer you if you wish to learn all about these death and burial customs. For the purpose I have in view I will here only quote a note of his. Eluku is described as the God Iraye born, offspring of the Royal House of Oniloku. "Oniloku" is the title of the monarch of Iraye, an ancient royal town. In one of the existing Jebu towns a descendant of Oniloku has lately been installed into that office in the Iraye quarter of the town.

There is a similar secret society in Calabar called Egbo and I have been informed by "Harry Hartze," the only European member, that it appears to him to be a modified and simpler form of Freemasonry. There are nine degrees and the cost to obtain the right to wear the peacock's feather, the sign of the highest grade, is about £70. I could not, of course, ask this famous African trader to tell me any of its secrets, but he assured me there was nothing phallic about it.

The noise made by the Egbo is done by means of a leaf and the Egbo's mouth, and when Egbo thus announces himself women and non-Egbos have to keep out of the way. The Society was formed for the purpose of aiding the chiefs to keep their slaves in order.

But the Poro Society, so ably described by Mr. T. J. Alldridge in his interesting book, "The

[1] *Nigerian Chronicle*, to be seen at the Royal Colonial Institute.

Sherbro and its Hinterland," does appear to be phallic, and a boy has no real name until he goes to the Poro bush, when it is given to him at his circumcision.

The dress of the Poro boys is very like that of the Nkimbi in the Congo (see page 127); it also appears to be a system of Freemasonry. The meeting for initiation takes place in the dry season and there are three degrees. But when Poro approaches a town he does not wear a distinctive dress. Upon the news of his coming reaching the town all men who are not of the Poro order, together with all women and children, must conceal themselves inside their huts and drop down the mats before the doors and window spaces. The women are to kneel down indoors, and clap their hands.

The heads of the Poro are called Tasso, they wear an enormous head-gear like the Ovia men of the Bini, the Eluku of the Yoruba towns in the Kukuruku Country (see page 209, *At the Back of the Black Man's Mind*), the Egungun of Yoruba, or the Mbundu of Kakong.

If a Tasso dies in a town he must not be interred there, and no woman must look upon a dead Tasso. But a woman can become a Deh-Boi or Poro woman.

In neither of these two foreign secret societies is anything of their origin known, but they rely on the superstitious fears of the people for their power.

III DEATH, BURIAL AND DEPARTED SPIRITS

I have shown that the Oro is certainly a secret society founded on the fear, so inherent in the native of Africa, of the actions of the departed spirits, and we have learned that the Ogboni is a kind of Executive Council which uses "Oro" as a deterrent, much in the same way as the Congo people and, in some parts of Yorubaland, the Yoruba use their fetishes.

In the making of a fetish (page 93, *At the Back of the Black Man's Mind*) I have described how one of these fetishes is made; the Nganga, with a number of people, goes into the bush and cuts a Muamba tree down, and calls out the name of the man whose Kulu or spirit shall inhabit the fetish. The man whose name is thus called out dies, and it is the fear of the harm which the spirit of this man may do that causes the fetish to act as a deterrent.

Westermarck in Chapter XLV, page 535, of his *Origin and Development of the Moral Ideas*, says: "The Basutos maintain that their dead ancestors are continually endeavouring to draw them to themselves and therefore attribute to them every disease, and the Tarahumares in Mexico suppose that the dead make their relatives ill from a feeling of loneliness, that they, too, may die and join the departed. But the notion that the disembodied soul is on the whole a malicious being constantly watching for an opportunity to do harm to the living is also, no doubt, intimately connected with the instinctive fear of the dead, which is in its turn the outcome of the fear of death."

The Bavili give their dead the most imposing funeral they can, and they bury their dead in places set apart for the purpose. The Yoruba, however, always buried their important departed in their houses and set apart a day in every year to do them honour.

The Yoruba seem also to connect ideas with which they have surrounded natural phenomena with personages whose characters seemed to them to fit in with these impressions, and then on the death of these persons to have deified them and gradually to have looked upon them as the cause of the effects produced by these natural phenomena.

Thus the darkness before dawn they looked upon as the beginning of the things that followed. It was harmful to them because they could not see.

Some person learned in Genesis they called Odudua, and on his death this person was deified, and as an "Orisha" became the Creator out of whom all things were made.

Again, their history tells us that "Shango," their lightning Orisha, was the fourth Alafin of Oyo and explains how he became deified.

But I will allow the native, as nearly as I can, to continue to tell his own story, and to convince you that whatever his methods, instinct or inspiration coupled with natural observation has led him to the foundation of a remarkably interesting mythology.

To conclude, we have thus far noted that Egungun is the *Father* come from heaven.

That Oro was the Orisha of the *first father*.

That Eluku was the offspring of the Royal house of

III DEATH, BURIAL AND DEPARTED SPIRITS 59

Oniloku. And on the death of Ogbola, a famous hunter near Olokemeji, I witnessed the women coming, stamping and singing Epa! Oro![1] Baba lo l'oni o! Baba wa l'amwa, awa kori o! Epa! Oro! We are looking for our Father! and we do not see him!

However much then the stories and their explanations may differ, enough has been said to allow us to conclude that the beatification of their ancestors is a very ancient custom of the Yoruba.

With this fact fixed firmly in our minds we can now proceed to consider their more developed Social and Religious systems.

[1] May not Oro be a contracted form of Ore-o and simply mean the spirit of the departed (father)—Adesola writes : Now *Oro* worship is undeniably spirit-worhip. Every *Oro* is itself supposed to be the Manes of a deceased parent or ancestor to which prayers and sacrifices are offered, and invocations made.

[NOTE.—I should like to remark in passing that West African secret societies seem to fall under three heads, *i.e.*, phallic, medical, and funerary. To the second class belong such organisations as the Leopard Society described by Aldridge, *loc. cit.*, the object of which is to obtain human kidney fat with which to make powerful medicine. These societies have only by degrees and at a later stage acquired political powers.]

CHAPTER IV

THE FOUR GREAT ESTATES IN THE NATIVE FORM OF GOVERNMENT

THE death of the founder of the family, presumably the grandfather, caused a great impression on the father, mother and son who were left, and I think I have said enough to show that the Yoruba reveres and beatifies his dead. The family that once was composed of three, *i.e.* father, mother and son, now became one of four, *i.e.* the Orisha (the departed father), and the father, mother and son. The father fished, the mother gathered vegetables, and the son hunted. It was the duty of each one of this little family to see that the Orisha was fed. In this way perhaps commenced the Yoruba first division of time into weeks of four days, the Orisha's day, the father's day, the mother's day, the son's day, and it was probably rather owing to the necessity of supplying the needs of the Orisha than their own humble wants that the necessity to exchange products first arose, hence the Orisha's day became the market day.

As the family became more numerous and developed into village life we find that the woman has fallen out of what one looks upon as her place and that her room has been filled by her brother in the family council. The head of the village now worships the village Orisha through the spirit of his dead father for his people, and is helped in regulating village affairs by the counsel of his wife's brother and his son.

Later on in Town life we find a further development, *i.e.* a kind of quadruple control composed of the dowager Queen mother or Iyalode and her Court, the Oba, and his Court, the Balogun and his Court, and the Bashorun and his Court.

(1) The dowager Queen's Court is now composed of :—

> (*a*) Three women named respectively Oton who proposes where meetings shall be held, Osi who goes round gathering information which she reports to the Iyalode, and lastly Ashipa who collects money and distributes it.
>
> (*b*) A Bale who acts as Iyalode's interpreter with Bada the chief of her messengers.
>
> (*c*) Small boys called Amade.

(2) On the other hand we have the Oba attended by three courtiers jointly called Igbi but respectively Oton, Osi, who hold up his right and left arms, and Jaguna the captain of his bodyguard and executioner. As these three are always near him they wield (or did so) very great power.

Barbot, in his "Coast of Guinea," book 3, chapter 27, page 290, mentions the names of three men as great Chiefs of the Court of the King of Fetu. (1) Dy, a high treasurer, (2) Brasso or standard bearer, and (3) the Fataira. On page 479 he says, "The Jagos have three governors, Singe, Kobak and Kabango."

In Benin city the Oba had three great ones, Onegwa, Offade and Arribon, whose titles appear to have been (1) Osuma, messenger connected with the King's wants (2) Esogban, messenger connected with King's gifts and (3) Esawn, the King's captain.

(3) The next great officer of state is the Balogun or war chief whose Court in Abeokuta is composed of Seriki, Bada, and Ashipa and their attendants.

(4) Then comes the Bashorun (the Iayse of the Bini) who is head of the Council and is attended by the three officers of the Council called the Ogboni, about which something has already been said and of which much more will be written.

Thus out of the simple government by the Grandfather (who became the Orisha) and father, mother, son, we have arrived at the development of a government by four great chiefs, each the head of a court of three and their followers.

(1) The Iyalode the relict of the grandfather.

(2) The Oba the father representing Fatherhood.

(3) The Balogun representing the brother of the mother or Motherhood.

(4) The Bashorun representing Sonship.

Nefftzer has called the Roman Gods the supernatural magistrates of the republic. We shall, I hope, be able to show that these four great chiefs have also their counterpart in heaven.

It is interesting and very important to note that

these four great ones fall into their places as pairs, Iyalode and Balogun, the female duality, and the Oba and the Bashorun or the male duality.

Bishop Johnson has said or written that so far as his studies go he can only find duality among the (so-called) heathen Gods. Now while the Dualities are plain enough, the puzzle is to find the Trinity.

May I offer the following as the solution.

Iyalode represents the mother in the past, the Balogun as the brother represents the wife of the King, the mother of the son.

The Oba equals the Father.

The Bashorun the Son.

In heaven the Orishas,

(1) Odudua represents the Creator in heaven or the Iyalode on earth.

(2) Obatala the Balogun, the mother's brother or Motherhood.

(3) Jakuta Fatherhood, and

(4) Ifa the Sonship.

Among the Bini the days of the week are said to be (1) the Regent's or Iyase's day, (2) Osuma's day, (3) Esogban's day and (4) Esawn's day. Among the Yoruba they are not only connected with the Oba and the three great chiefs but they are called Odudua's day, Jakuta's day, Obatala's day and Ifa's day.

Thus the Orisha's (or market) day is now known as Odudua's or Iyalode's day, the father's day has become Jakuta's day, the mother's day has become Obatala's day, and the son's day has become Ifa's day. Thus altogether there are two dualities, a female and a male.

One person of the female duality belongs to the past and the Trinity is represented by the father, mother, son, Jakuta, Obatala and Ifa or the Oba, the Balogun and the Bashorun.

I will now proceed to say something more of these great Orishas whose names are now known to us.

CHAPTER V

JAKUTA. THE FOUR WINDS

Jakuta

THE Yoruba have confused Jakuta with Shango until they are to-day almost identical, but there is in reality a difference between Jakuta the great "procreator" and Shango, the son of Yemoja, the so-called god of lightning and the great marriage deity.

Jakuta may be said to be Shango in a former period, and Shango is to-day worshipped on the day called Jakuta.

Jakuta as the thrower of stones, so closely connected with Odudua who may be said to represent chaos, is rather the thunderbolt than the lightning, and was looked upon as the great father in heaven.

He is likened at times to the east wind, the cause of the coming of the thunderstorm with its clouds, rain, and wind connected with the first tornado season. At this time the ancient Yoruba's (father's and son's) thoughts turned to marriage, and no doubt in the fights that took place stones were the weapons that they used. And now a stone fell from heaven. Ah!

thought the stone throwers, the dead father in heaven is also at war and throwing stones, and so perhaps came the name Ija strife, Oko stone, Ta[1] to produce, shortened into Jakuta. The verb Ja is to fight, and okuta is a stone.[2]

I remember travelling behind Chilunga, now in Congo Français, and coming across a large stone near to the top of a hill which had marks on it. These my companion Tate told me were the foot-prints of God (Nzambi).

At Adenyoba on the Osse River, or rather in the bush not far from there, a large stone is venerated in the same way by the Bini.

---

[1] Also to throw.
[2] The verb Ko is to grow hard.
    Oko is a stone,[3] also a farm.
    Oko bo is a eunuch.
    Oko the foreskin.
    Oko a husband.
    Oko a hoe.
    Oko a spear.
    Ako beginning.
    Ako a male.
    Ako obiri a strumpet.
    Iko where the pillar is and where they meet, comes to mean a meeting.
The verb Lo is to engraft.
    Lu is to bore.
    Olo is a millstone.
    Olu is a hammer.
    Solu is to copulate.
The verb Le is to engraft.
    Ole is embryo.
    Ile means land, a town.
    Ilu a nation.

---

[3] Oko, a farm, is pronounced in the same way as oko, a stone, with change of intonation, but oko, a husband is pronounced awkaw, in the same way as oko, or awkaw, a hoe.

V   JAKUTA. THE FOUR WINDS

Monsieur P. Saintyves in his book *Les Vierges Mères et les Naissances Miraculeuses* has given us a long account of fecund stones, so that we know the Yoruba is by no means alone in his veneration of sacred stones.

If Togun had not remarked that Ajaguno was a woman, I should be inclined to say that Jakuta and Ajaguno were one and the same person, and that Jakuta was the power that did the fighting for the greater gods, as his name is always coupled with theirs as in the names of the four days of the week.

But it must be remembered that Jakuta really represents the Spirit of the departed Father, the stone-thrower who has gone to heaven and who rules through his son on earth.

At the time when Jakuta was worshipped as the dead father in heaven the Yoruba had not yet developed the ideas now connected with Olorun (the owner of heaven).

These ideas must have come to them when, or rather some time after, they had come to dwell in towns. It seems that Jakuta is the first step in the development of the Yoruba idea of God. Jakuta (or rather now they say Shango) is said to have been a King or Alafin of Oyo, the typical and temporal head of the Yoruba race. (See *Yoruba-speaking Peoples*, page 50).

It is most interesting to read in a description of South Guinea by Barbot (page 306), in writing of the natives of the Gold Coast : " When it thunders they say it is the voice of the trumpets, or blowing-horns of Jan Goeman, so they call God, who, with reverence be it spoken, is diverting himself with his wives; and, therefore, when it thunders much, or though there be only flashes of lightning, they presently run under cover if possible, believing that if they did not so God would strike them with his *thunderbolts*.

"About the year 1480, the Spaniards trading at the coast found those blacks extremely covetous and fond of a sort of seashell, giving anything they had for them, as believing they had a peculiar virtue against thunder. Whereupon so many of those shells were carried out of Spain that at last they were scarce to be had there for money."

Bosman, writing about thunderstorms, says: "The stake which supported our Flag was shattered int splinters from top to bottom, and yet remained standing, but so torn asunder as if one or two hundred chisels had been driven into it in order to split it. The negroes, in the same terrified condition, with us being of opinion that the force of the thunder is contained in a *certain stone*, after the storm was over brought one, which they ridiculously believed had so shattered our Flag pole. But no wonder they were of that opinion, for in Europe, where we think we are better informed, several people don't much differ from them." Then he goes on to say, " But what I have observed of the effects of thunder is sufficient to convince me that 'tis impossible they should be caused by a stone." All I have to say to this is "Jakuta!"

The Four Winds

The East in Yoruba is known by the name of Ila Orun, *i.e.* the place where "he that arises appears."

Ila also means the act of splitting, possibly the idea comes from the fact that here darkness and light become divided. This idea of splitting brings their thoughts to creation, written Ida, and this word again can be traced to the verb Da to be and to make or Ta to produce, as yams are produced by splitting up the seed yam.

This meaning coincides with the Bavili word (see chapter Obatala, page 82) Xivanga or Creator, Va meaning to split.

Ila also means Salvation, and we know that both the Yoruba and the Bavili say that their religion came from the East.

The West is Iha Igun aiye ibuwo, the corner region of the earth (where the Sun lodges). It is interesting to note while talking of the West that it is to the South-West of Ife, the supposed centre of the Yoruba Kingdom, near the beach or where the Sun sets, that we find the Ifa sacred palm tree in large quantities, said to have been first found in Orungan's farm or where he lodged. Orungan is another name for Orun the Sun, that is the heat of the Sun at midday.

The North is known as Ari Wa Otun Ila Orun, one who finds and comes to the right of the East.

The South, or Igun kerin aiye, is the fourth corner

of the world. It is evident then that the Yoruba idea of their world was that it was square and that the sun travelled from the Eastern corner to the Western corner. Their proverb, "Igun Merin ni Aiye Ini," says, "The world has or is supported by four corners." This probably explains the figure marked in chalk on the ground in front of the altar to the Orisha Olokun (the sea spirit) noticed by me at Igo near Benin city (see chapter XXI, page 225, *At the Back of the Black Man's Mind*). The mark is ⊠. The native places his back to the East and looks westward and so has the North on his right. The Yoruba also have a figure called Olori merin which has four heads, which is generally found placed upon a mound near the centre of the town so that each head faces one of the four great points of the compass. Four times every year a new-born infant four days old used to be sacrificed to this power in the presence of its mother. Colonel Ellis calls this sacrifice Ejeodun, the season of blood, and tells us that while Olori merin protected the town and watched the four points of the compass from his mound it was believed that no war or pestilence could attack it. Now a force of men attacking a town would come by the roads and try to enter the city by one or all of the four gates, but sickness and pestilence, the Yoruba say, are brought by the winds.

This dual attack may be described as a personal and physical invasion, and as the gates are in the centre of each wall while the points of the compass are

JAKUTA. THE FOUR WINDS

the four corners of the walled town, the following figure may be said to represent these ideas. The only

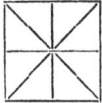

one of the four great Orishas connected with the winds is Jakuta, translated roughly as the Hurler of Stones, the Yoruba Jupiter. He comes with the East wind that brings tornados. It would seem to follow that the four Orishas, Jakuta, Obatala, Odudua and Ifa should represent the East, North, South and West winds.

I have been informed by Babalawo Oliyitan that the figure Olori Merin is not in itself an Orisha but merely a Juju representing the above four great Orishas, and as it has been stated that this figure faces the four points of the compass and guards the city from pestilence and war we can assume the position of each Orisha.

Looking towards the West Obatala will point to the North, Odudua to the South, Jakuta to the East and Ifa to the West.

The Yoruba calls the winds that bring disease Afefe Buruku,[1] Buruku being another name for Shankpana, the small-pox "god," who is said to be a son of "Yemoja."

But on the other hand Oliyitan tells me that a whirlwind, which he called Aja, carries people off to the bush, and, keeping them there two or three months,

[1] Afefe buruku means bad or ill wind.

teaches them the use of medicinal herbs by which diseases are cured.

Olorun (Awlawrun) is the word now used for God. Olu means owner, Orun heaven or sky. Jakuta, we have noted, is the Father God, the stone-thrower connected with the wind that blows the mysteries of the East to the centre of the Kingdom or the walled city. The Sun (Orun) rises in the East; it is possible therefore that the wind and storm god as a spiritual revealer is nearly related to the Sun as the physical revealer, and I think we can understand, as religious ideas developed, how Olorun took the place of Jakuta as the heavenly Father God and how Jakuta under the name of Shango became a mere marriage Orisha.

CHAPTER VI

ODUDUA AND THE FOUR DAYS OF THE WEEK

TOGUN said Orishala was the husband of Yemuhu, but Ellis tells us that Obatala was the husband of Oduduwa. Are we then to suppose that Yemuhu and Oduduwa are two names for one person, or that Orishala had two wives? I am inclined to believe that Oduduwa and Yemuhu[1] are two names for one person. Bishop Crowther also gives this deity the name of Odua. Bishop Johnson talking of the Odus[2] in Yoruba heathenism says, " Behind each one of these representative nuts are sixteen subordinate divinities. Each one of the whole lot is termed an Odu, which means a chief, a head." Bishop Crowther gives the word Olu as the chief of anything.

Oduwa and Oluwa then mean the same thing, *i.e.* " Owner," which in the form of Olowa Ini or Oloni is now another name for God. Bishop Crowther also says Odua or Odudua is a goddess from Ife, said to be the supreme goddess in the world. Heaven and earth are also called Odudua—

---
[1] Ye means " Mother," and Muhu is to cause to be, to cause to germinate.
[2] Ifa's sacred palm nuts.

"Odudua Igbá nla meji adé isi. Heaven and earth are two large calabashes which being shut can never be opened." And Ellis says Obatala and Odudua, or Heaven and earth, resemble, according to the priests, two large calabashes which when once shut can never be opened. . . . He goes on to say, according to a myth Odudua is blind. In the beginning of the world she and her husband were shut up in darkness [1] in a large closed calabash, Obatala being in the upper part and Odudua in the lower. . . . Odudua complained to her husband of the confinement. . . . In a frenzy Obatala tore out her eyes. . . . She cursed him and said, "Naught shalt thou eat but snails." It will be remembered that Yemuhu's snails became the sixteen heads of Eleda, or, in other words, the sixteen Orishas taking part in the creation of the world. The calabash or gourd in which Odudua was confined is called Igba. The words for ancestor are "Obi Ara Igbani, the parent body in the time past," and in this sense it is interesting to read in the *Nigerian Chronicle* an article on the history of the Yoruba by one signing himself F. S.

"At the head of immigrants who settled in Yorubaland about the eleventh or twelfth century of the Christian Era was Odudua from whom most of the present day native rulers are descended. Odudua, however, was not the real name of the leader of the Bornu immigrants. His name, together

---

[1] The verb Du is to be black. Dudu means black. Odudua is the goddess in darkness and blind opposed in a sense to Obatala who loves that which is white, clear and light.

with those of his wives and children and companions are entirely lost, and his descendants many ages after his death designated him Odudua, *i.e. Odu ti o da wa*, which means a "self-existing personage." He is also called *Adumila* ("Saviour"). His wife, from whom are descended the dynasties of the leading Yoruba kingdoms, was designated Omonide, *i.e. Omo ni ide*, which means a "child is brass,'" brass being the most precious metal known to the early Yoruba people. Omonide is also called *Iyamode*, a contraction of *Iya Omonide* "Mother Omonide."

Odudua is worshipped in every Yoruba town, and every Yoruba man, woman or child is called *Omo Odudua* ("child of Odudua").

Many years after the death of Odudua a Hausa Mussulman came to Ife. He used to call the inhabitants together and read to them passages from the copy of the Koran which he brought with him from his country. He was wont to say to the people in Yoruba imperfectly as he could speak it with accents foreign to the language—*E wa e je ki a sin Allah, On ni o da oke, On ni o da ile, On ni o da gbogbo nkan, On ni o da wa* ("Let us worship Allah, He created the Mountain, He created the lowland, He created everything, He created us"). He did this from time to time without being able to gain a single proselyte, and died a few months after his arrival in Ife. After his death his Koran was found hanging on a peg on the wall where he had left it in a bag. Some of the men who saw it said *Hausa ti o ku ni so fun wa pe Odu ti o da iwa ma ma ni eyi o, eyi ni Odudua, e je ki a ma bo o.* ("The late Hausaman told us this was the personage who created existence,[1] this is Odudua, let us therefore worship him"), misunderstanding the Mussulman. So they removed the bag containing the Koran from the peg on the wall, put it on the ground, covered it with a pot and began to worship it. So commenced the worship of Odudua.

Odudua had by Omonide, his first wife, several children; his eldest daughter was the mother of the founder of Owu, who become king of Owu, and was consequently styled Olowu. All the children of Omonide were famous, and became founders of several towns in the Yoruba Country. The names of Omonide's children or of any of the children of Odudua are practically lost. Omonide's eldest son founded Ketu and became the Alaketu or king of Ketu. Another founded Benin (Ibini) and became the Onibini. Another founded Ila (Igbomina) and became the Onila. Another founded Sabe and became the Onisabe. The youngest of Omonide's children founded a town, the habitable portion of which was so small that it was called Kogbaye ("It does not afford room"), of which he became king. Owing to the smallness of this town the inhabitants left it stealthily, hence it was said that they slipped off the place. They went to a locality not very distant from Kogbaye and settled there. Their king also went and remained with them. From the circumstance of the people slipping off (*yo lo*) from Kogbaye the new settlement was called Oyo ("slipper"). The youngest son of Mother Omonide thus became the Oloyo.

Odudua himself died in Ife, and one of his children

---

[1] Odudua is by some regarded as a contraction of *Odu ti o da iwa* ("the personage who created existence.")

by his other wives was given a broom wherewith to keep his grave clean. This child was made the Oni or king of Ife.

The Alaketu, the eldest son of Odudua, was the first of his sons to take a wife. His wife soon had a babe and Mother Omonide, who had hitherto remained at Ife, came to help her son's wife in nursing the babe. This babe afterwards founded Ake and became the Alake. Mother Omonide loved her grandson very much and came with him to Ake, where she died."

We shall have a good deal to say about these sons of the founder of the Yoruba Kingdom. It will be noted that F. S. calls Odudua a male, whereas Ellis, Oja, Togun, and Crowther speak of her as a female.

Upon asking people the question, who first gave the days of the week their names? I have always been told that Odudua inspired them. The names of the days of the week were first given to me by Oja in the following order :—

        Eshu.
        Orishala.
        Odudua.
        Jakuta.

This was at Ilobi, South-west of Egbaland. An old lady called Tinnawe living near Olokemeji gave me the days in the following order which she said had been inspired by Odudua :—

>Awo. Ifa's day.
>Ogun.
>Jakuta.
>Obatala.

Oliyitan[1] gave the days and names as follows :—

>Awo.
>Ogun.
>Jakuta.
>Orishala.

Ellis gives the first day as a day of rest, but gives no name for it, and then the following.

>Awo or Awu.
>Ogun.
>Shango, another name for Jakuta.
>Obatala.

The differences apparent in the above list are (1) Eshu for Awo. Awo is the day set apart by the priests of Ifa to renew the chalk marks made on the earth in front of the altars of the Orisha. As Eshu the devil shares all the sacrifices made to Ifa, it is called Ifa's day—Eshu's day, or the day of Awo or mystery.

Shango worship has taken the place of the worship of Jakuta in some places, but Shango has been described to me as the servant or son of Jakuta who attends to the lightning. Again Shango is a son of "Yemoja" who is the daughter of Obatala.

---

[1] A priest of Ifa.

Ogun is a son of Yemoja and has become a very important power as the "god" of iron and patron of hunters. Here we have a minor power, as a part, usurping the place of Odudua as the earth goddess who was the first protector of hunters, much in the same way as Shango has taken Jakuta's place.

Orishala and Obatala are one and the same.

An Ibadan named Moredaio gave me the days in the same order, so that I think we are justified in looking upon Oja's order as wrong, but in this case Odudua has her right place, *i.e.* that of Ogun in the other lists.

Another reason for Ogun taking Odudua's day may be that very often Obatala and Odudua are spoken of as if they are one. As Ellis put it, "according to some priests Obatala and Odudua represent one androgynous divinity, and they say an image, which is sufficiently common, of a human being with one arm and one leg, and a tail terminating in a sphere, symbolises this." This being so, the part of the earth Ogun may have come to take Odudua's place.

The four days of the Yoruba week, then, are: *Jakuta's day* which is looked upon as a Sunday. On this day they clean their houses, and rub their floors. Then they "split" Kola for the Orishas Shango, Yemoja, Oshun and Buruku.

Obatala's day, sometimes called Orishala. On this day they rub the walls and floor of the houses, and fill a pot of water on the altar; and when they eat they give part of their food to him. The following "white" Orishas are worshipped on this day :—Larun. Ijaiyi, Iluofun, Ijemdori, Ogiyan, Alajugun, Owa Olufon. These white Orishas are appealed to by barren women, and they must not be offered palm oil or pepper.

Awo, or Ifa's day. The people cannot consult Ifa except through a priest. In this way he is consulted about everything. On this day the Ifa priests renew the chalk marks on the ground in front of the altars.

Oshun and Odu are also consulted on this day. I have more to say about Ifa later on.

Odudua's or Ogun's day. When they build, or clear a farm, or cut a tree, or hunt they split kola to Ogun. Ija and Oshowsi are also worshipped on this day. Odudua representing the creation, it is quite natural that they should consider her day as first in their week. The first, the fifth, the ninth and seventeenth, which they look upon as the beginning of a new month, are sacred to Odudua, and are all market days.

In Benin city there are four markets, one of which is called the "Queen Mother's market," and this, as we have already seen, is the position of Odudua.

CHAPTER VII

OBATALA

Four Gates

THE literal meaning of the words Obaba Arugbo, the other name by which Togun told me Orishala is called, is Father Greybeard.

Orishala, Bishop Crowther says, is another name for Obatala, whom he calls the Great Goddess (?)[1] of the Yoruba, the framer of the human body in the womb. But Togun called Orishala the man, the husband of Yemuhu.

The word is evidently formed of the words Orisha and nla.

Ellis says the word Orisha seems to be compounded of Ori (summit, top, head) and Sha (to select, choose), though some natives prefer to derive it from ri to see, and isha choice, and thus to make it mean one who sees the cult. Bishop Johnson says these deities are generally known among us as Orishas, and that they were spoken of as "Awon ti o ri sha," *i.e.* those who were successful in making their collection of the wisdom strewn about by the son of

[1] Mine R. E. D.

God. But it is more likely that the word is composed of Ore departed spirit, and Isha one who is chosen, selected or cut off, or, in other words, the beatified departed one. Among the Bini the word Orisha is pronounced Oyisha,[1] a compound of the word Oye a title of honour expressing wisdom of the elders,[2] and Isha, one who is chosen. La in this word Orishala has the meaning of to split.[3]

Oba, in Obatala, the other name for Orishala, is also a title of honour, meaning Emperor, King. Ta means to produce as yams are produced from split seed yams. There is therefore little or no difference in the meaning of the words Orishala and Obatala, and, as Bishop Crowther says, Orishala and Obatala are one.[4]

Orishala.

A story told me by an Egba called Salako shows that Obatala as a god is the person who sensitises matter :

"He is the son of Odudua, and was sent to do good on earth. When anyone is sick he

---

[1] Oye may be derived from Yeye Mother, while Oba may be shortened from Baba Father, so that Oyishala and Obatala may be the female and male form of the same idea. The word Orisha and Oyisha is, however, used in much the same sense as the word Nkici (plural Bakici ba ci among the Bavili, which I have translated as the speaking powers on earth. The late Bishop Crowther translates the word as deity, gods, idols.

[2] Compare Kulu in the Congo.

[3] I may point out that the idea of splitting, separating, is also connected with the idea of Creator in the Congo—Xivanga = one who keeps on splitting, or Creator. Orishala may be a dialectical form of Orishanla Orisha and nla ; nla being an adjective meaning big or great.

[4] See his Vocabulary and Dictionary of the Yoruba language.

will tell them what leaf to get and they will get well. If any woman wanted a child, any leaf he cut and gave to her would have the desired effect. Then the people thanked Odudua for sending him, and said he was a good man. Then Odudua made the body of man and called Obatala to do the rest, and so Obatala made the fingers, the eyes, the mouth, the ears.

They who worship him used to call him Obatala to da oju, imu, eti, emi, ati apari shikokanlelogun—Oba who makes the eyes, the mouth, ears, nose, and the skull to be, twenty-one.[1]"

When he finished the work, Olodumare breathed into the body and it became a living being. And so Odudua gave orders to all the world to worship Obatala, and those who now worship him are the descendants of those who benefited by his goodness when he came on earth. And now he is Odudua's mason and sculptor.

All things that Obatala and his followers wear are white—white chalk, beads, cap and cloth.

Mr. Pellegrin gave me a story of Obatala as a person or King; he said :—

"Obatala was the poorest of the four Kings; he bought an Albino as a slave. And when famine was raging he had nothing to eat, and he had a wife and child; so when they were starving he told the Albino to go and find his own chop.[2]

---

[1] I believe the numeration of the Yoruba to be a kind of summary of the Orishas and their attributes.
[2] Chop = food.

He went crying about the streets. He stood at the gate of the town, as some people with food might be coming. That day a European with his retinue came accompanied by a dog. The dog, who came first and met the Albino, was frightened and ran back to his master. The master came to find out what had frightened the dog, and found the Albino at the gate. He asked him what was the matter, and he told him his story. Then the European asked him to take him to his master. And he asked Obatala why, if he had food for his wife and child, he had none for his slave? The master told him of the famine, and said he had sent the Albino to find his own 'chop.' Then the white man, seeing their condition, mixed some milk for them and stayed that night. Next morning when going he gave them food and money, and left. Obatalaka[1] called the slave to come and count it. But they did not dare to touch it, as it was too white,[2] so they took a matchet to divide it, hence silver is called Fadaka.[3] After this Obatala became the richest of all the Kings. The white cloth they wear to-day is owing to the coming of the saviour whiteman. The milk they mistook for palm wine, so they do not drink it.

They do not eat dog because he was the means of pointing out the Albino."

In the olden days each great town was enclosed

---

[1] Obatalaka means the master of a poor man.

[2] See page 89, where Obatala is said to have made the brain, nerves and skull, or the white parts of the body. The dark part, *i.e.* the blood and flesh, are evidently the part Odudua created.

[3] Fa to shave, scrape ; Da to be scarce, hence a time of dearth ; Ka to take a quantity out of a soft mass.

within four great walls in the same way, as the Yorubas say, that their kingdom was ; and leading out of the city were four great roads (God's roads, as the Bavili called them), which passed through four great gates. The Balogun, or war chief, is the guardian of these on earth, and Orishala or Obatala is said to be the spiritual Balogun and protector of these gates.[1]

The mother among the Bavili, and also the Yoruba, acts as a kind of Treasurer. She guards the wealth of the family. In the case of the town, the war chief, representing motherhood, guards the wealth of the town from pillage. It would seem as if Orishala (the female form of Obatala) referred to the mother in the oldest form of parental government, and that the name was altered when the family had increased and multiplied, and the mother's brother had, under the name of Obatala, taken her place in the developed Council.

[1] The names of the gates at Abeokuta are now :
Bode Alafinwa.
,, Shodeke.
,, Owu.
,, Aro.

CHAPTER VIII

IFA AND THE FOUR WALLS OF THE YORUBA KINGDOM

OJA through Togun told me that Eleda fought with Ifa, in consequence of which he became a hearing speaking, seeing, thinking being, and that this sensitising of Ifa was accomplished through Obatala. Bishop Crowther translates the word Eleda as Creator, Supreme Being. Ellis says it is another name for Olorun, the Yoruba sky god, in his capacity as the controller of rains.

The literal meaning of Ele is "a piece patched on," and da means to make, which seems to back up Togun's statement that Eleda was a creative power told off to perform the perfecting of Ifa. Bishop Johnson tells us (see Appendix, *At the Back of the Black Man's Mind*) that Ela is another name for Ifa, although the name is often used as if it represented a separate and distinct divine personality. From this it would appear that the word Eleda is composed of Ela and Eda, Ela meaning a piece severed from a larger piece, and Eda the making; thus Eleda would mean not God, but the act of making Ifa or Ela, the word Ifa meaning a piece that is scraped off or created.

CH. VIII IFA AND THE FOUR WALLS OF YORUBA

Ifa is the first-born or Oni[1] of Odudua and Obatala. He is known by the names Awnomila, the calabash in which the sixteen sacred palm nuts are kept, the name, also, that Oja gave for the sacred stones at Ife; Akpani ebora ynagiddi Odudua, or Odudua's private secretary, Elerin ipin, or one who laughs; Afo yo manitaw; or a man who shakes his mouth but does not speak.

He is the Oracular[2] deity about whom most is known, and who is most often consulted. A very good descripton is given of him by Colonel Ellis in his "Yoruba-speaking People," page 56, and by Bishop Johnson in his "Yoruba Heathenism," and many of his wise sayings are to be found in Bishop C. Phillips' book called "Ifa."

That Ifa's Councils are god-like can be inferred from the following quotation of one of his sayings given by Adesola in the *Nigerian Chronicle* :—

> E so'tito e se rere
> Eni so'tito ni imole i gbe
>
> Be faithful be good
> For the faithful and good are favourites
> of the gods.
>
> Olotito ab'ona tororo
> Osika ab'ona gbarara
> K'eni ma seke
> K'eni ma dale
> Odale bale ku
> Eni dale a bale lo

---

[1] Ifa calls the first-born Oni, the one who has; the second-born Ola, the saviour; the third Otunla, the day after to-morrow; and the fourth Kokoro Kundu Eru Oni.   [2] See Chapter XV.

> Narrow yet straight is the path
> of righteousness.
> But broad and many-sided are the ways
> of the wicked
> In purpose be thou true
> Not given to perfidy
> For the work of the perfidious will o'er-take him
> The evil of the wicked shall slay him.

Ifa as head of the priestly government of the Yoruba is the greatest Orisha or Nkici, the priestly King in Heaven, who, as the first Oni, is the priestly King (or Nkici'ci) on earth. The following legends describe him as a great prophet on earth:—

Mr. Oyesile Keribo,[1] in a Yoruba pamphlet published in August, 1906, on the History of the Gods, writes on Ifa (page 19) to this effect:—

"Ifa was a native of Itase, near Ife country, and of poor parentage: in his youth he had great aversion to manual labour and therefore had to beg his bread. To better his condition he applied to a sage for advice, and the latter taught him divination, traditional stories with matters relating thereto and medicine as an easy means of obtaining a livelihood. He afterwards became very popular. The sixteen original Odus correspond with the sixteen original stories taught to Ifa, etc. His parents being poor were not known in the country, hence he was afterwards considered to be without parentage and deified after death."

---

[1] Mr. Keribo's pamphlet was printed by the Egba Government Printing Press (August 22, 1906), and widely circulated at 6d. a copy there and in other parts of the Yoruba country.

VIII IFA AND THE FOUR WALLS OF YORUBA

In the *Nigerian Chronicle* of March 12, 1909, writing on *Ifa*, Mr. F. S., a correspondent of that paper, says:—

"*Ifa* was born at Ife, the cradle of the Yoruba people. He was a skilful medical man, who had an extensive practice and was an eminently successful diviner.

After he had become famous he founded a town called *Ipetu*, and became king of the place and was styled Alapetu.

He was very popular, and was regarded by his contemporaries as a true prophet. People from every part of the Yoruba country flocked to him and patronised him. His fame was so great that hundreds of persons from different towns begged him to admit them as disciples and apprentices under him. Out of these, we are told, he chose only sixteen men from about as many different towns—from Ekiti, from Oyo, from Ijebu, and many other places widely separated.[1] The names of these apprentices or disciples are said to be identical with the names of the sixteen divinitatory signs called *Odus*, and the order of precedence among them, which was probably based upon priority of appointment, is said to be still preserved in the present order[2] of the *Odus*."

An intelligent native called "Ifebode" gave me the following story about Ifa:—

"Ifa was a human being who used to make medicine, and sell it. While doing this he got to Ife, and made that his headquarters. One day all

---
[1] See Chapter XV.
[2] This is most important. See Chapter XV.

the Ife people joined together to fight him. Then he got vexed and went into the earth, and when they asked him to come out he refused unless they agreed to worship him. The day he entered the earth he cut four palm leaves to mark the place, and they each immediately became a palm tree— each tree had four branches, or sixteen in all. He told them to pick sixteen nuts, which he said they must worship, and ask him whatever they wanted. From then, anyone who got these nuts became a Babalawo and became diviners, and these nuts teach him what leaves to pick to cure any sickness.

The Babalawos at Ife wear cloths of light blue."

We have noted that one of Ifa's names is Awnomila, and that he was the first Oni, that the present Oni of Ife called the pillar of stone, which Oja called Awnomila, the stick of Oranyan, the first Oni of Ife. Now the word Oraniyan[1] means "a matter of dispute," so that we may conclude that there is some dispute as to the first Oni's name.[2]

In a later chapter we shall discuss the names of the Odus, or 16 + 1 sacred nuts of Ifa, which we only mention in this place because the number of the sons of the first Oni is said to be 16, and the number of his daughters 1, or 16 + 1 offspring.

A hunter, said to be a priest of Ifa, was introduced to me by Mr. J. T. Palmer, a native trader residing at Sapele, and the number and names of the offspring of the first Oni, Oranyan, given by him were confirmed

---

[1] Crowther writes the word Oraniyan or Oroiyan (see his Dictionary, page 231).
[2] We should say Mr. What's-his-name.

VIII IFA AND THE FOUR WALLS OF YORUBA

by my friend Oliyitan, another priest of Ifa, three years afterwards, at Olokemeji.

The hunter said that the Oni was suffering from some eye complaint, and thought he was going to die, so he divided all his goods amongst his children and ordered them to go to certain villages and live. Alafin was forgotten, so he was given all the land owned by the Oni.

The present Oni of Ife showed me the door through which on another occasion the future King of Benin City passed when he was sent away to occupy the land of the Efa.[1] And he stated that Ilesha was not sent out for a long time after his brothers, because the Oni of that time loved him, and wished him to be near to him.

In all matters referring to land, the Alafin takes the place of his progenitor the Oni, and the present positions of the two great Yoruba chiefs, Alafin and Oni, are equivalent to those of our King and of the Archbishop of Canterbury.

The list of the names is as follows :—

(1) Alafin, the youngest son, the head of the Oyos, the owner of the Palace, the one who takes the place of the Oni in mundane affairs, the head of the officers of the Council[2] or Ogboni.

(2) Olowu, from whom the Egbas are descended, who, as an officer, may have represented the treasurer.

---

[1] This custom of the Kings' sons being sent out to govern provinces has been handed down and strictly adhered to by the Bini.

[2] See Chapter X. on Yemaja and the Ogboni.

(3) Awujale, from whom the Jebus are descended, who, as an officer of this ancient Ogboni, may possibly have acted as executioner.

(4) Alaketu, from whom the Ketus are descended, and who, in this Ogboni, appears to have acted as the arbitrator.

These four great ones, the officers as it were of the first Ogboni, are compared to the complete Yoruba Kingdom, which they say was enclosed by four walls. Their saying is Igun merin ni ile ini, a house is composed of four corners (*i.e.* four walls), and is not otherwise complete.

We find in Abeokuta four kings, the Alake being at present the paramount chief, so that I conclude that each of the above four great ones, composing the Yoruba Kingdom, took three other sons of the first Oni with him. I regret to say that I cannot say who the three were in each case, so that I must leave this matter in the hands of some future historian, but the names of the Councillors or sons are as follows:—

> Obalado, the founder of Ado, where Ifa is said to have been born.
> Oba Baruba, the founder of Barita, a town north of Ilorin.
> Oni Moba, said to be another name for Shango.

These three possibly accompanied the Alafin.

> Oluhu, said to be one of the four Kings of Egba land.

VIII IFA AND THE FOUR WALLS OF YORUBA

Owa } said to be part of Ifa's talk.
Ore }

Oba Shabi, possibly the founder of the county in Ketuland, where Orungan had his farm, and from where Ifa is said to have procured his sixteen sacred nuts.

Ajeru, Ifa's messenger.

Orogun, to do with divination.

Ewi u Osoin, an Orisha said to speak in a small voice.

Ajank Moba, part of Ifa's talk.

Alara, the owner of thunder.

The Babalawo Oliyitan described all the above as parts of Ifa, and as among these parts we find the ancestors of the Oyo, Egba, Ijebu and Iketu (the four walls of the Yoruba Kingdom), the connection between Ifa, the first Oni, and the walls is self-evident.

It is very difficult to separate Eshu from Ifa, as we have noticed in considering the days of the week, so I will now tell you something about this personage.

CHAPTER IX

ESHU

ELEGBA and Eshu are translated Devil. In the form of an earthenware pot with a hole in it, Eshu is represented in many villages. In some form or other under a small shed, Eshu is found at the entrance of a town or house. Whatever Orishas the people may have, Eshu appears to be the most widespread (see *At the Back of the Black Man's Mind*, pages 197, 190, 221, 223, 234, 246, 265).

The first blood of a sacrifice is generally splashed over Eshu, so that he may not prevent the Orisha to whom the sacrifice is made from accepting the offering.

I think the explanation of the fact that the native looks upon the number of Orishas as 201 or 401 is that Eshu possibly has the same number of malevolent Orishas as Ifa has of beneficent.

I have pointed out in *At the Back of the Black Man's Mind*, page 197, that Eshu represents the procreative trinity, as opposed to the spiritual Oyisa. (see also chapter on the Odus of Ifa, where Odu is the name of the sign of the new moon called Oshu).

Eshu[1] is the Being of Darkness, while Ifa is the Being of Light and Revelation, personalities whose signs are Oshu the new moon and Orun the sun.

At Akure some people came dancing up to the resthouse where I was staying holding palm branches in their hands and beating drums in a violent way. I asked them what they were doing. They answered that they were sacrificing to the devil. Well, I assured them, "I am not the devil." They laughed and ran away, leaving me rather in doubt as to whether they thought me so or not. On inquiry I heard that in three days they were going to keep the feast of Ifa, and that preparatory to doing so they had to feast Eshu or the devil.

The three Phallic pillars at Iaiu were called Eshu (See *At the Back of the Black Man's Mind*, page 195). Ellis tells us "He is supposed always to carry a short knotted club, which, originally intended to be a rude representation of the Phallus, has partly through want of skill . . . . and partly through the growing belief in Elegba's malevolence, come to be regarded as a weapon of offence. . . . The rude wooden representation of the Phallus is planted in the earth by the side of the hut, and is seen in almost every public place, while at certain festivals it is paraded in great pomp, and pointed towards the young girls, who dance round it."

It was Elegba who told Ifa where to go for the sixteen palm nuts and who taught that personage how

---

[1] See note, Chapter VI., and note, Chapter X.

to divine,[1] and he stipulated that in return for this instruction he should always be allowed the first choice of all offerings. This possibly accounts for Eshu getting the first part of the blood of every sacrifice.

Eshu

As the story goes, Odudua has no other Orisha except Ifa, and, whenever he [2] consulted anyone, he consulted Ifa. Ifa came one day to sacrifice to Odudua, and he was very satisfied with the offering. As it is a rule when a chief is pleased with the services of a person to give him something, so, on this occasion, Odudua gave Ifa Eshu. Thus Eshu was the slave of Odudua, and became Ifa's messenger. And when anyone wants to sacrifice to Ifa they say that it is best to square his messenger,[3] as he is a wicked person.

[1] See appendix *At the Back of the Black Man's Mind*, page 270.

[2] Odudua is here spoken of as he, and if we remember that Odudua stands for the Dowager Queen Mother and so for the ancestor her husband this confusion is easily understood.

[3] Opele (See *At the Back of the Black Man's Mind*, page 233) is spoken of as Ifa's messenger and offspring.

CHAPTER X

AGANJU, YEMOJA, THEIR OFFSPRING, AND THE OGBONI OR COUNCIL

THE Bashorun is not only one of the four great chiefs, but also the chief officer of the Council of State or Ogboni.[1] We may expect, therefore, to find that Ifa is not only one of the four great Orishas, but also the chief officer of the godly Council of Orishas. And so it is except that here Ifa is represented by Eshu.[2]

Aganju and Yemoja are said to have been the offspring of Odudua and Obatala, and it is related that they had a son called Orungan. These then are the three officers presided over by the great procreative Orisha Eshu. And it is interesting to note that here again we have the formula of four, Eshu representing the past, and Aganju, Yemoja and Orungan, the Trinity of Father, Mother, Son.

Aganju is sometimes described as a younger brother of Jakuta, but very little is known about him, except that the word means " Space " or " Expanse."

---

[1] Ogboni is both the society of that name containing many members and also the council and offices of the King's cabinet.
[2] See page 100, Chapter X.

Yemoja a great River Spirit (the mother of the shining light) is the mother of Orungan, the heat of the sun at mid-day (passion ?).

Orungan is known as Fi rin pon na yanju omo Yemoja—The son of Yemoja (who) cleans his eyes (with) a hot iron, or Erin re bi ija omo Oba Afeleja— His laugh is like fighting the son of the King who fights with the sword (or Ogun).

Yemoja, or Ye mo aja, is the most important perhaps of these three, as from her sprang the twelve or thirteen Orishas forming the deified Ogboni or Council.

Yeye means mother, and Aiye means earth; Mo is to shine, and Aja is short for Aja-Osu, a name by which the dog star is known, whereas Orun is the name of the sun or day star. Thus we get the picture of earth, mother (of the) shining star or sun.

Now Orungan (Ellis[1] tells us) "fell in love with his mother, and, as she refused to listen to his guilty passion, he one day took advantage of his father's absence and ravished her. Immediately after the act Yemoja sprang to her feet, and fled from the place wringing her hands and lamenting, and was pursued by Orungan who strove to console her by saying that no one should know of what had occurred, and declared that he could not live without her. He held out to her the alluring prospect of living with two husbands, one acknowledged, and the other in secret, but she rejected all his proposals with loathing, and continued to run away. Orungan, however, rapidly gained upon

[1] See Ellis, *Yoruba-speaking People*, p. 54.

X AGANJU, YEMOJA, THEIR OFFSPRING

her, and was just stretching out his hand to seize her when she fell backward to the ground. Then her body immediately began to swell in a fearful manner, two streams of water gushed from her breasts, and her abdomen burst open. The streams from Yemoja's breasts joined and formed a lagoon; and from her gaping body came the following offspring."

Before we continue our study of Yemoja's offspring I should like to interpret this story of creation as far as we have gone in my own words.

I do not think it follows that because there is such a sameness about these stories of creation that they must necessarily be different variants of any acknowledged version. "Great minds think alike," the saying goes, and in this way great men in many parts of the world still come to much the same conclusions. The intelligent Yoruba is, however, constantly discovering resemblances in his laws, customs and folklore to that of the Old Testament; it may therefore be well, without changing the natural order of the Orishas, to point out where their ideas, though differently expressed, evidently refer to the same phenomena.

Odudua   has been shown to express the ideas of self-existence, heaven and earth, darkness, and so as a heading may easily be made to stand for "In the beginning God made heaven and earth .... and darkness was upon the face of the deep."
Jakuta   has been connected with thunder, and so electricity. "And the Spirit of God moved

Obatala	upon the face of the waters" (or white[1] vapours), just as Fatherhood and Motherhood meet in marriage. Obatala, though a male personage, it must be remembered, stands for maternity.
Ifa	Ideas of speech and revelation and light are connected with Ifa—"And God *said*, Let there be light: and there was light."
Eshu[2]	The personality connected with darkness: "And God divided the Light from the Darkness."
Aganju	Expanse, space. Ferrar Fenton in his translation of Genesis instead of the word "Firmament" uses the word "Expanse"—"And God said, Let there be an 'expanse' between the waters and the waters and let it be for a division between the waters and the waters."
Yemoja	is a great water spirit as well as mother earth: "Let the waters below the heavens be collected in one place, and let dry land appear."
Orungan	the heated rays from the sun which produce —"Let the earth produce."

The Yoruba has only four days in his week, and we find that each day is dedicated to an Orisha.

In the first place we have God separating from himself two great persons to help him in Creation.

[1] White is sacred to Obatala.

[2] In Eshu's other name Elegba we have the words gba to strike with a stick, Ela another word for Ifa, meaning that which is stripped or split off. In each of the three parts we have a division or splitting off—light from darkness, division of waters and waters, land from water.

Arranging these personages and phenomena in sets of fours in the manner in which the sons of Oranyan were arranged, we have :

Odudua	Jakuta	Obatala	Ifa
Eshu, Devil Dudu, black light	Aganju, space Orun, heaven	Yemoja Aiye, earth	Orungan Imole,
Oshu, new moon	Omi, water	Ile, land	Orun, sun

From this it will be noted that the sun and moon fall into the fourth line, but I do not think the native would say that the sun and moon were made on the fourth day, but rather that they were manifestations of Odudua and Ifa in the fourth place.

To return to the Ogboni of Orishas, Ellis gives the list of Yemoja's offspring as follows :—

Dada	god of vegetables
Shango	,, lightning
Ogun	,, iron and war
Olokun	,, sea
Olosa	goddess of the lagoon
Oya	,, ,, River Niger
Oshun	,, ,, ,, Oshun
Oba	,, ,, ,, Oba
Orisha Oko	god of agriculture
Oshosi	,, hunters
Oke,	,, mountains,
Aje Shaluga,	,, wealth,
Shankpana	,, smallpox,
Orun	the sun, and
Oshu	the moon.

From this it is seen that Ellis gives Yemoja as the mother of the sun and moon. I have made many inquiries about this, and none of my informants have included them in their lists of the offspring of this Orisha. And from what I have written above I think it is clear that the sun and the new moon, as personalities, are Ifa[1] and Eshu. Neither have I ever been able to get anyone to agree with the order given by Ellis. The names, however, of the other Orishas agree with those I have collected.

The names and order, so far as I have been able to discover, are :—

{ Olokun, the owner of the sea which murmurs.
{ Olosa, owner of the lagoon which evaporates.
{ Ogun, the one that pounds.
{ Oshowsi, the enchanter that is.
{ Oke, the one who cherishes.
{ Shango, Lightning.
{ Oshun, the one who gathers together.
{ Oko, the one who collects.
{ Oya, the one who plucks.
{ Shaluga, who elevates, enriches.
{ Oba or Ibu, the one who bakes or boils.
{ Buruku (or Shankpana), to rot, to die, and
Dada, the Orisha of birth.

As I have travelled nearly all over the Yoruba country I have obtained the order of sacrifice to Orishas in towns widely apart, and now give them to show how far the worship in these different places agrees, firstly as to the Orishas worshipped,

[1] See figure, page 150, Chapter XV.

AGANJU, YEMOJA, THEIR OFFSPRING

and secondly as to the order in which their festivals are kept. As some fourteen years have passed since Colonel Ellis wrote his *Yoruba-speaking People*, it is possible that some changes have taken place, not only in the original order, but also in the number of local Orishas, or it may be that local traditions have been too strong, and that the order in which the Orishas set apart by Ifa as the offspring of Yemoja to be worshipped has never been fully adopted.

The following are the lists as given to me in a few important towns.

	Akure.	*Isehin.*	*Awaye.*	
1.	1 Alla.			
2.	2 Oshun.			
3.				
4.				
5.				
		(1)	(2)	
6.	3 Ifa.	11 Ifa.	19 Ifa.	
7.	4 Iweshu.	12 Elegba.	20 Shango.	
8.	5 Agbarigbo.	13 Yemoja.	21 Orisha Oko.	
9.	6 Olokun.	14 Oshun.	22 Obatala.	Rainy Season.
10.	7 Idala.	15 Shango.	23 Yemoja.	
11.	8 Aiyarigbi.	16 Orisha Oko.		
12.	9 Oile and Oloba.	17 Oke.		
13.	10 Ibegun.	18 Orishaula.		

[1] and [2] See chapter on the Seasons and the original division of time which only took note of the Rainy Season.

	Egbados.		*Ife.*		*Oyo.*
24.	Shango.	35.	Orishala or	48.	Egungun.
25.	Orisha Oko.		Ole.	49.	Shanpona.
26.	Oshowsi.	36.	Alashe.	50.	Oke.
27.	Oshun.	37.	Orisha Teku.	51.	Kuku.
28.	Ogun.	38.	Ogara.	52.	Shango and
29.	Ifa.	39.	Okun.		Oya.
30.	Orisha Oko,	40.	Ifa.	53.	Ifa.
	wife.	41.	Ogun and	54.	Orisha Oko.
31.	Shapana.		Oranyan.	55.	Eynile.
32.	Olofin.	42.	Mori mi.	56.	Yemoja.
33.	Yewa.	43.	Oranfe.	57.	Oshun.
34.	Eserikika.	44.	Odudua.	58.	Eshu.
	No sacrifice.	45.	Ojumo.	59.	Orishaula.
	do.	46.	Iro.	60.	Oro.
		47.	Ikeri.		

It is possible that in the last three lists two Orishas are worshipped every lunar month, or one every seventeenth day during the rainy season.

It is evident that at the present day there is no order common to the different sections of the Yoruba people, as Ifa is about the only one to whom they sacrifice at the same time, *i.e.* at the beginning of the rains, or about the sixth month.

We have now considered the four supernatural great chiefs and the four supernatural officers of the spiritual Ogboni, and given the names of the offspring of Yemoja, who evidently form the supernatural Ogboni or Council.

Before describing these Orishas more at length I think it will not be out of place to give a complete list of the names of the officials in the native Government.

The names of the officers are as follows :—

1. Iyalode, the Queen Mother.
2. Oba, the King.
3. Balogun, the War Chief.
4. Bashorun, the Prime Minister.
} Four Great Chiefs.

5. Bashorun, the President.
6. Apena, the one who convenes the meetings.
7. Oluwo, the Treasurer.
8. Adofin, the Arbitrator.
} The Officers.

The Council.

9. Lisa, one of the Iwarefa.
10. Egbe Iwarefa, or assistant Iwarefa.
11. Bisa.
12. Assistant.
13. Bala.
14. Assistant.
15. Asalu.
16. Assistant.
17. Malakun.
18. Assistant.
19. Ashipa.
20. Assistant.

These last fifteen members of the Government are called the Ogboni, composed of three officers and a Council of six Iwarefa and six assistant or Egbe Iwarefa, but there are many members of the Ogboni as a society.

I will now show how the offspring of Yemoja are connected with the life and occupation of the Yoruba.

CHAPTER XI

OLOKUN OLOSA AND FISHERMAN

Fishing

As we approach the coast of Africa from Europe the first Africans we meet are fishermen. It is true that we seldom get near enough to the tiny fishing canoes to see much of the fisherman, but then he is far from us and sometimes out of sight of land. The sea in some places is dotted quite thickly with the canoes of these venturesome natives, whose courage and manliness we must all admire. Confined as we all are on board even the most comfortable of steamships nearing the end of our trip we almost envy the fisherman his freedom and loneliness. He has left the coast early in the morning with the land breeze and when the calm sea is rippled by the coming sea breeze he hoists his little sail and returns to his home.

As we pass these crowds of specks upon the ocean we feel that this sort of thing has been going on for centuries and that the earliest foreigner to approach these shores must have been equally touched .as ourselves on our first contact with these hardy inhabitants of the Black Continent.

OLOKUN OLOSA AND FISHERMAN

Barbot evidently took a great interest in fishing and fish as connected with the natives of the Gold Coast, and in his *Description of the Coast of South Guinea* writes :

"At my first voyage, whilst we lay before Conimendo, some fishermen, near our ship, took a fish about seven feet long. . . . The Blacks call it Fetisso, but for what reason I cannot determine unless it be to express that it is too rare and sweet for mortals to eat and only fit for a deity. . . . As I remember the Blacks would not sell it but only allowed me the liberty of drawing its figure. . . . I am apt to believe the Blacks look upon this fish as a sort of Deity ; though I did not hear they paid it any religious worship. If they do, there is nothing new in paying adoration to a fish ; for the Philistines in the first ages of the world adored Dagon, which was an idol half man half fish : the word Dagon in their language signifying a fish : and that those Gentiles looked upon as the great god, Judges xvi., 23. 'Dagon our God hath delivered Samson our enemy into our hand.' Dagon represented Neptune the God of the Sea and by him perhaps was meant Noah. The Syrians according to Cicero and Xenophon, adored some large tame fish, kept in the river Chalus, and would not suffer any person to go about to disturb them. The Syro-Phœnicians according to Clemens Alexandrinus, adored those fishes with as much zeal, as the Elians worshipped Jupiter : and Diodorus Siculus affirms the Syrians did not eat fish but adored them as gods. Plutarch mentions the Oxindrites and Cynophites, Egyptian nations which having been long at war about killing a fish they esteemed sacred, were so weakened, that the Romans subdued and made them slaves."

One feels inclined, after reading this, to exclaim " Dear old Barbot ; " for we can so fully enter into the spirit which seems to have permeated the minds of the great African traders of olden days, and which, in spite of the rush of this day of steamships and railways, still influences so many of us.

The Kings of Benin had to be supported under each arm by two chiefs whenever they attempted to walk because they claimed to be descended from such a deity as mentioned by Barbot (see plate XVII. Antiquities from Benin in the British Museum), and by way of proof they say that one of their Kings "Ehenbuda" by name was born with legs with no bones in them. Perhaps in reference to this myth the late Mary Kingsley wrote: "The manners and customs of many West African fishes are quaint. I have never yet seen that fish the natives often tell me about that is as big as a man only thicker, and which walks about on its fins at night in the forest, so I cannot vouch for it."

When in due course we land on the beach in Africa we find fishing is of a more sociable nature, for here we see numbers of men and boys launching their great nets in canoes and casting them into the sea four or five hundred yards away on the far side of the surf. Having left the end of a grass rope, attached to one end of the net, in the hand of a small boy, on the beach, the fisherman in the canoe after discharging the net brings in the rope tied to the other end with all possible speed. As the canoe rushes merrily through the surf and almost before it grates upon the sandy beach willing hands seize the rope, and, together with those who have now gone to the help of the small boy, begin to haul the net and its contents to the land.

A fishing beach is not a pleasant place to walk about on, unless the sea breeze is strong enough to blow the stench of half cured fish away from you. Barbot's words of nearly 150 years ago may be said to still stand good in many places where he writes (page 42, "Description of the Coast of Nigritia"): "It is very unaccountable that these people, having such plenty of several sorts of large fish, will not dress it while fresh and sweet, but let it lie buried along the shore; especially the pilchards, as I suppose to give it a better relish or else that it may keep longer. In short, whether this be any particular fancy of theirs or that the continual violent heat immediately corrupts it, this is certain, that they eat none but what stinks, and account it the greater dainty. To instance somewhat more particularly, as to pilchards, they only let them lie some days buried in the wet briny sand along the shore, and perhaps it may be on account of its saltness; but afterwards dig up and expose them to the sun for some time to dry; and then lay them up in their huts which are all the day like stoves; and thus they daily eat and sell them to the inland blacks who come down to buy them, to supply the country markets. I have seen whole cabins or cottages full of these dry pilchards at Rusisco, and the sand down before it next the sea so stored that there was an intolerable stench about the place."

The great sea Orisha of the Yoruba people is called "Olokun." The Benin river is called after him and the Bini say that he married when poor the spirit of the river Oha which runs into the Olokun near its mouth.

His second and favourite wife, however, was the Sapoba river called by the natives Igbagon (see *At the Back of the Black Man's Mind*).

The Lagos people who were governed by chiefs crowned by the Oba of Benin, say that Olokun married Olokunsu or Elusu who lives in the harbour at Lagos. She is white in colour and human in shape, but is covered with fish scales from below the breasts to the hips. The fish in the waters of the bar are sacred to her, and should anyone catch them she takes vengeance by upsetting canoes and drowning the occupants. (See Ellis, *The Yoruba-speaking People*).

When the sea is rough and the people cannot fish they say Olokun is angry. In the olden days the people would then sacrifice a human being to appease his wrath and so be able to fish, but as a rule his wrath seems to have been calmed by offerings of animals and foodstuff.

In Bishop Phillips' *Ifa* Odu No. 3 Ejiogbe, the Oracle is made to say: "All the honours of the waters upon earth cannot be as great as the honour of the sea. All the rivers that have their source above are not so beautiful as the Lagoon."

The sea Olokun is said to be in the first place the Lagoon Olosa in the second as Orisha.

Many kinds of nets and traps are used by the fishermen in the Lagoons in Africa and it is a pretty sight on a bright day to watch the busy fishermen at work, some in canoes patiently fishing with hooks, some throwing a round shaped net, an importation from Accra, some busy arranging their traps, and others on the beach dragging the shallows for small fish and prawns.

Olosa the Orisha of the Lagoons looms large in the mind of the pagan fisherman and when floods prevent his operations he concludes that she is annoyed and offers some sacrifice at one or other of the many altars erected in her honour along the banks of the Lagoon. Human sacrifices, it is said, used to be offered to her, but she is now satisfied with animals and vegetable products.

Crocodiles are her messengers and Ellis tells us " Food is regularly supplied to these reptiles every fifth [1] day, or festival, and many of them become sufficiently tame to come for the offering as soon as they see or hear the worshippers gathering on the bank."

But leaving the Lagoons and entering the mangrove banked rivers everyone will have noticed the shy fisherman in his tiny canoe perhaps spearing fish and have passed his wife carrying her baby on her back just as she wildly steers her canoe out of your sight up some tiny creek.

These fishermen live in small bamboo huts some-

[1] The 5th day is the first day of a new week and is Odudua's day.

times built on piles in a surrounding swamp and sometimes on the sandy bank of a river in the midst of a sea of grass. A solitary lonely life it must be.

And now we come to where the river passes through country more or less cultivated and governed by some responsible chief, and we find that certain fishermen have fishing rights along specified reaches of the river with a number of fishermen under them.

In this district (Olokemeji) this head fisherman is called " Baba Olodu," Father or owner of the river. All fishermen under him are supposed to give him part of their catch, and he in turn is supposed to give the Alake of Abeokuta, in whose Kingdom we live, a certain quantity or its equivalent every year. There are two such Baba Olodu near to Olokemeji, Akitunde and Idowu by name, and it is from them that I have obtained the following notes.

Anyone may fish, but if a stranger fishes he is supposed to give the Baba of the district part of his catch. They have four kinds of traps :—

1. The Kolu, a net-like trap made of the tie-tie or native rope or string known as Agba. When the fish enter this trap the float above is pressed down.

2. Ogun called Owa, a trap made up of the leaves of the palm tree which is used in both large and small streams and is left in them all night and examined in the morning.

3. Koko, a trap made of Agba and placed in large and deep rivers. A string is tied to the trap and fastened to a shrub on the river bank, and when the shrub shakes they know a fish is in the trap.

4. Agbagba, a trap made of Egburo or Awkaw tie-tie. This is for shallow rivers and is placed between rocks with its mouth just above the level of the water, and fish coming over the fall drop into it.

Before the fisherman starts to fish he gets a pod of pepper, atare, and places it in a hole on the bank of the river, he then puts seven grains of corn on the top of this. This is to secure good luck. If his catch has been a success the fisherman makes a thank-offering to Yemaja or Yemoja, the mother of Olokun and Olosa. He fills a pot with cooked maize and on the top of it places seven kola nuts. He then pours palm wine, or corn beer, or gin over the whole and puts it into the river. Yemaja is said to carry this offering to her offspring.

In going to fish if he stumbles and strikes his right foot no matter, but striking his left foot means bad luck. This sign is called Akilo.

When the bird Kowe crys or sings Krrr it is a good sign, but if it is silent it is looked upon as a bad sign.

Another man will know his luck by the quivering of his eyelid. The quivering of the left eye-lid is a sign of a death in his family.

The time for fishing in the interior is the dry season and best just when the rains cease and the rivers begin to fall.

Although fishermen have in this district their head man or Baba Olodu, they have no guild or secret society like the hunters. (See next chapter.)

When a fish black in colour, with two horns in its

head, called Aro (the owner of the river) is caught, it is quickly returned to the river. (This is, perhaps, the copper fish (*Ostracion quadricornis*). Its young, however, may be killed. Then the Abori, fish with one horn, are sacred to Yemoja.

They do not like catching the Ojiji (*Malopterurus electricus*), as they say, when large, they can kill a person; and the Adede, called "Owoternu" by the Lagos people, does not please them, as they say that when full he turns the waters black.

This life of the fisherman is perhaps the most simple and wanting, from its solitariness, perhaps, in organisation. We are, perhaps, nearer to what we may imagine primitive life to have been in this study of the life of an African fisherman than in any other. But primitive as it may be, the fisherman thanks his god, Yemoja, for his good luck, and knows that sin, such as theft or adultery, is hurtful to his luck.

A Flood Story.

(According to Ellis, page 64.) Sometime after settling at Ado, Ifa became tired of living in the world, and accordingly went to dwell in the firmament with Obatala. After his departure, mankind, deprived of his assistance, was unable properly to interpret the desire of the Gods, most of whom became annoyed in consequence. Olokun was most angry, and in a fit of rage he destroyed nearly all the inhabitants of the world in a great flood, only a few being saved by Obatala, who drew them up into the sky by means of a long iron chain. After this ebullition of anger, Olokun retired once more to his own domains, but the world was nothing but mud, and quite unfit to live in, till Ifa came down from the sky, and, in connection with Odudua, once more made it habitable.

Thus are Olokun and Olosa the first offspring of Yemoja and Orungan connected with the category "water" and the occupation of the fisherman.

CHAPTER XII

OGUN, OSHOWSI, AND THE HUNTER

ONE catches glimpses of the rule by father form of Government in Africa in a fisherman's or hunter's camp, often a long distance from any village, they live solitary camp-like lives. The fisherman's life we have described; the hunter smokes and dries the product of the chase and exchanges this for other necessaries of life in the nearest market. He is more or less governed by his senses and his desires, but he believes thoroughly in his Orisha "Ogun." He accumulates a certain amount of goods and as he desires to marry he invests his capital in obtaining a wife. They have children and the result is a hunters' village. Other hunters ask his permission to share his hunting-grounds and on certain conditions he allows them to do so. These hunters in all probability marry the head hunter's daughters.

The men hunt and the women do the marketing and cook for their husbands. Men living in the wilds of Africa facing death in numerous ways become what some people call superstitious and others religious.

This may account for the fact that most of the old

CH. XII OGUN, OSHOWSI, AND THE HUNTER 117

Coasters, though they were not credited with leading a religious life but rather a kind of unlicensed patriarchal one, were generally found to be believers in their Bible and could always produce one when needed.

Now the hunters in Africa are nearly all thorough believers in their Orishas, and before going out on their expeditions in Yorubaland they offer kola nuts to the Orishas Eshu, Ogun and Oshowsi. Their great time for hunting is when the grass has been burnt and it is then that the greater sacrifices are offered. In the district of Olokemeji no human sacrifices were offered to Ogun, so Agbola's son told me, but, he added, in other districts human beings used to be killed. He said that when a hunter goes out he sacrifices to the three above-named Orishas ; they kill a cock giving Eshu a dash of its blood, and then leave it at the foot of Ogun's altar. After a while they come back and take the bloodless body of the cock away and eat it, they also give Ogun kola. To Oshowsi they give roasted beans, and just before leaving on a small hunt a hunter throws pieces of a kola nut into the air and as the pieces fall upon the earth, so he knows he will have good or bad luck.

A second good point about the hunter is respect for the head hunter and obedience to his commands. Having rubbed his body all over with soap mixed with some powder, and placed chalk marks on his head so that animals shall not smell him, he presents himself before the head hunter and tells him where he is going to hunt, so that there may be no overlapping. Should one hunter meet another on his way he salutes him and walks on in silence, and should he omit to tell the head hunter where he is going to hunt, or then shoot somewhere else than in the appointed place, the head hunter will take his gun and money from him and cast him out of the camp.

If one hunter tries to poison another he will meet with no luck.

If he commits adultery he will have no luck, and if while away hunting his wife commits adultery he will see a male and female animal copulating. If he loves his wife he dare not shoot either of these creatures, since, if he killed them, his wife would die. So he goes back at once to his town and taking his wife before Ogun's altar accuses her of the sin. If she admits her guilt, the adulterer is fined one dog to be sacrificed to Ogun, one goat for Ifa, and three bags of cowries together with kola for the husband. But if she denies it they ask her to take some of the kola from Ogun's altar, and if she eats the kola (being guilty) Ogun in two or three days (unless she confesses) will kill her. Sometimes a ram will run after her and butt her to death.

And when the hunter cannot kill anything and he hears the nightjar crying in the day he knows something has happened in his town and he returns to Ogun knowing that some relation is dead or very ill. Or when the bird that cries " Ko! we! " and then " tche! tche! " cries " Ko! we! " three times without adding " tche! tche! " he knows someone is dead.

But supposing a man has had a woman illicitly, he

AGBOLO'S SONS. GREAT NATIVE HUNTERS.

[*Face p.* 119

XII OGUN, OSHOWSI, AND THE HUNTER

takes a big snail, some shea butter and the leaves of the Odudun, Tete and Renren, and pounding all together (after first sacrificing to Ogun), smears his whole body with the mixture and goes his way rejoicing knowing that all is well.

Should a hunter happen to kill an animal that is pregnant he makes an offering of one dog, palm oil, and kola to Ogun.

If a hunter tells a lie he will kill nothing, and if two hunters have gone before Ogun and sworn to keep a thing secret, and one then goes and reveals it, some animal will fight with him and may kill him.

And when a hunter knows that he has not committed any of these crimes, and still has bad luck, then he knows that Ogun wants a present.

I have often had to spend the night in one or other of these primitive fishermen's and hunters' villages, and in the morning when I have asked to see the "Father" to say good-bye to him I have been told that I must wait if I wish to see him as he has gone to the grove sacred to Ogun, to pray for his people.

And so the hunter believes in his Orisha and obeys his father's will and knows that he will be punished for any offences against the divine and human father's will.

Agbola's son told me that there are strong beasts in the bush such as leopards, elephants, lions, chimpanzees, unicorns (?), bush cows, etc., and that when a hunter shoots at one of these he immediately sprinkles a medicine called Kaji in front of him in the direction of the animal so that it will not get up and charge him.

Hunters, he said, do not believe that men can turn themselves into leopards, but they do believe that certain people called Ologun have the power to influence these beasts and so cause them to kill people. Hunters protect themselves against this risk by buying and wearing a belt with medicine in it called Ishora. Their ancestors gave them the prescription according to which these belts are made.

The leopard in this country is known by the names Ekun, the fearless one, Ogida the one ready to scratch, and Jakumu the striker. An Ibadan hunter told me that the leopard represents the land, and that the Alafin alone could call himself "the Leopard," because he inherited all the land from the first Oni of Ife.

The Alafin's warriors, called Kakamfu, who, by the way, number 201 [1] (the original number of Yoruba Orishas, or rather the number said by the priests of Ifa to have been in the right hand division), used to wear an apron of the leopard's skin.

When the leopard was killed its face was covered with a cloth (a custom they have in common with the Bavili) because, as the hunter said, it is a king. The king is not supposed to look anyone in the face for fear of frightening him.

The Leopard king, or Alafin, is known by his crown of blue beads, six marks on each cheek, Orania's sword (Ida orania), and a calabash wrapped in cloth called (Ibayiwa), a stick covered with beads

[1] The Yoruba heathenism, *At the Back of the Black Man's Mind.*

called Okpaleki, and he does not wear a necklace, whereas his chiefs do.

Elephant-hunting regulations in the Benin Kingdom.
The hunter wants to kill an elephant.
1. He goes to the King and asks permission.
2. The King gives him a boy.
3. The boy stops in the village, the hunter goes into the bush.
4. When he kills the elephant he comes and tells the King's boy what he has done.
5. The hunter then returns to cut up the elephant.
6. The leg nearest the ground when the elephant falls is for the King.
7. The fore leg belongs to the village landowner.
8. The neck belongs to the hunter's wife.
9. The back round about the kidneys is for the King's mother, Iyoba.
10. The upper fore leg to the hunter's boy.
11. The upper hind leg to the hunter.
12. The head belongs to the village boys who accompany the hunter.
13. The two tusks and the King's leg are given to the King's boy.
14. Some of the meat that is over is given to the King's boy.
15. The hunter and the King's boy take the leg and tusks to Benin city.
16. The village paramount chief takes them to the King.
17. The King then takes one tusk and gives one to the hunter.

18. The hunter next states that he has no wife, the King then may give him a woman or not, just as he thinks well or not of the hunter.

One of the causes that influenced the King was whether the hunter always killed the large elephants and left the small ones.

The King kept his tusk either as a juju, or for a future present to a white man or some foreign chief who visited him.

Should a hunter kill an elephant without permission he would be arrested and fined.

"Obodo, Adji, and Oluku and others shot an elephant without a license at Ubogwi. They refused to come in, so the King sent Ogiromeci with plenty of boys to arrest them; one fought and escaped.

"When they came the King accused them of killing an elephant, and as a punishment sent some of them to Igwihollo and some to Igwinigbo to hunt elephants for him, and kept them there for three years.

"When the hunter (stranger) came he generally brought a present for the King, but before he could go before the King he had to 'dash' (make a present to) the paramount chief."

Hunters in Yorubaland have societies or guilds, and they appear to be of two kinds, the Egbe Omode an ordinary hunter's society, and the Egbe Oluri Ode which has its headquarters at Abeokuta.

Ogbolo of Olokemeji was one of the four great officers of the "Egbe Olori Ode," the other three residing in Abeokuta. The titles of the four are:—

1. Oyeshile, meaning the throne is vacant.
2. Bi eyi oku, If this is not dead.
3. Ojo, The afterbirth sticks to his head.
4, Ogbolo, meaning near the Ogun.

Their council is formed of six hunters and six assistants. Thus it would seem that the hunters with their great Orishas, Ogun and Oshowsi, have an "Ogboni" on earth, the members of which, we may presume, have their Orishas in heaven.

Ogbolo's son told me that the name of the first great hunter was Akoka, but that the Orisha Ogun first directed men to start hunting. He pointed out to them also his sacred trees, the Peregun, Akoko and Atori: and made them dig four holes and plant four sticks to uphold a kind of altar or shelf, upon which they place the heads of all animals they kill and where they also sacrifice dogs to Ogun.

Ogun after Shango and Ifa is perhaps the best known or most popular Orisha in Yorubaland, and this probably arises from the fact that in almost every village there is a hunter or a number of them.

One hears Ogun's name constantly and he appears to be the owner of some very potent medicine. As Ellis says, "Any piece of iron can be used as a symbol of Ogun and the ground is sacred to him because iron ore is found in it." On a visit to the Asehin of Isehin I was taken through various courts to the court where he holds his palavers. I was astonished to find goats, sheep, and women here, quite contrary to custom, and the place was filthy. Across this court from north to south an iron chain was tightly stretched and pegged down. Near the middle of this line was a stone newly covered with the blood of a dog that had been sacrificed. I asked what it meant and was told by the Asehin that it was Ogun medicine.

In the palace yard at Akure and also in one of the streets there are mounds of mud about three feet high on the top of which lie large flat slabs of wood and these they call Isi Ogun. They are sacrificial tables where dogs are, and at times human beings were sacrificed.

Ibegun, which is the name of the dog sacrificed, is also worshipped at Akure. It is strange how the companions of the Orishas are sometimes talked of as wives, sometimes as brothers. The following story given to me by Asani an Egba describes Ogun and Oshowsi as brothers.

Oshowsi.

Oshowsi and Ogun are two brothers, and when they were young they were very wicked, and were driven away from their home by Jakuta because they refused to acknowledge his authority. They became great hunters. The natives say that Oshowsi is Ogun's wife, but this is not so, they were both the sons of one father. Oshowsi used to go ahead and Ogun followed. Oshowsi's real name is Olu fu si, Ogun's other name was Ija, he that beats and fights the game that Oshowsi points out to him. Oshu osi[1] was a left-handed man. In this case Ogun and Oshowsi are connected with the category Earth and the occupation of hunting.

Ogun and the Blacksmith.

From the fact that the blacksmith has the same Orishas as the hunter it may perhaps be presumed that the necessities of the calling of the hunter have, at a much later period, brought his occupation into existence.

He is an industrious and interesting person, and does not like you to ignore him as you pass his smithy. Tang, tang, tang, strikes his hammer on his anvil as you approach, as if to say, "Here I am, a cheery good day to you!" and so you are invited to go up to him and return his salute.

The mysteries of heat and cold, and light and darkness have been revealed to him. He cannot, it is true, explain them in words to you, for to him each process is a mystery, and his language is still a poor one from the European's standpoint.

But he has observed, and the knowledge is his. See how the metal expands as it gets red hot and contracts as it gets cold, and how, when he thrusts the heated metal into water, evaporation and condensation take place. He has seen all this a hundred times. Again, heat dissolves and melts, and cold consolidates and solidifies. He notes this daily. Divided or broken bits of iron by heat and cold be-

---

[1] Oshu osi is contracted into Oshowsi.

come fused and conjoined and made hard. He watches the ebullition of the molten mass which, as it cools, subsides and passes from motion to rest. Activity, inertness, energy, pressure, sensation, numbness, light and darkness, are wonders that impress themselves upon his receptive mind as he day by day manufactures his hoes, knives, spear heads, and what not. It will not surprise us at a later period if we find in the philosophy of the Blackman an Orisha for each of these phases in a natural process.

After reading Barbot's account of the blacksmiths of his day in a description of the Coast of North Guinea it is pleasant to turn to Mr. C. V. Bellamy's sympathetic account of "A West African Smelting House." I cannot help quoting largely from this very interesting paper :

"Not far from Oyo, not more than three days' journey from the coast, there is a small village whose inhabitants have been engaged in the extraction of iron for generations past, and where the methods are the same probably as those practised by the earliest workers in this metal ...... They are simple and unsophisticated, but they practise an art which is unknown to the savage and which places them high above him in the social scale, while it entitles them to be considered to have reached a higher degree of civilisation than many of the tribes met with in European countries where the people have been looked upon as domesticated.

"The shale is excavated with the aid of a rude pick in pieces weighing from three to five pounds, and is carried to the works for treatment.

"They first roast it over a fire of green timber; this is done during the night; the next morning it is pounded in a mortar. The poundings are screened until there is nothing remaining in the mortar, the sieve consisting of a native made basket rather openly woven, and they are then borne away to the river side for the purpose of washing or panning . . . . The washed ore is conveyed to the smelting house and poured into the kiln as occasion may require, in a damp state."

For a description of the smelting house, the arrangement of the shed, and the cupola, etc., I must refer you to Mr. Bellamy's paper.[1]

"Probably the most remarkable feature in the whole of the process is the use of selected clinker for a flux. This may throw light upon what is now frequently a matter of doubt, namely, the medium employed by the ancients in their smelting operations.

"The pig iron, after it has cooled down sufficiently, is broken up into convenient lumps for the purpose of sale or barter." This pig iron is sold to the blacksmiths whose work Mr. Bellamy describes.

"The bellows consisted of a pair of circular wooden bowls about a foot in diameter, connected by an air passage constructed of the same, from which two wooden pipes to do duty for the tue-iron lead to the earth; over the top of each bowl is loosely secured an undressed goatskin, to which is fastened in the centre of the bowl a long bamboo rod, one of which is held in each hand.

[1] To be found in the Royal Colonial Institute.

"The skin is very slack, and by raising and lowering the rod alternately a more or less continuous current of air is supplied to the hearth. There is no inlet valve to these bellows, and the air supplied enters by the wooden tue-pipes, a space being left between the hearth stone and the nozzles for the purpose; the bellows and hearth rest upon the ground. . . .

"For heavier work a large smooth, undressed and water-worn stone does duty for an anvil, but for smaller work another anvil is provided like a silversmith's, made of metal produced locally. The hammers look at first sight like so many rude lumps of iron roughly handled with the same, but a closer inspection shows them to be systematically shaped and diamond-wise in section so as to expose a flat or an edged surface by a single turn of the wrist; it is an ingenious pattern. . . . With such simple means as these the smith puddles the iron which has been smelted after the manner already explained.

"These smiths prefer their native iron to the bars imported."

Mr. Bellamy continues, " Not the least important feature in this industry is the marked regularity which characterised each operation and the enthusiasm which seemed to inspire the workers. Strangely at variance with the usual custom of the Ethiopian, there was no noise, no bustle; no confusion; no sound but the hum of preoccupation was to be heard throughout the whole village; at the right moment the kiln was prepared, and lighted, sealed charged and drawn; at the right moment when the fire was drawn, little boys stood ready with their calabash trays to take away the live charcoal, and at the right moment they brought the necessary green creepers with which to draw the pig from the cupola, or water to quench the fire. All this indicated systematic control and the strong hand of authority, and method only acquired by long practice and passed on from one generation to the next."

CHAPTER XIII

SEASONS

IT is quite impossible to understand the philosophy of the African without some knowledge of his seasons. Meteorologically this is not very hard, at any rate, in a place like Olokemeji where the seasons are marked. A glance at the chart will be sufficient. It will be noted that the year is divided into thirteen lunar months. Many natives will tell you that there are fourteen months in their year, but this we will explain further on, we are now only considering the lunar months as they are looked upon by many followers of Ifa.

The Yoruba are now more or less skilled farmers and live chiefly on the products of their farms, so far as farinaceous food is concerned, but we know that there was a time when they were far more dependent on forest products. It is most remarkable how many semi-wild products the natives have to fall back upon which at one time their ancestors may have had to live on almost entirely. And a great advantage is that, as far as my knowledge goes, they are able to feed on either the leaves or the fruit of most of the undermentioned plants all the year round. The names of some of these are the Ogunmo (?), the Oyo or Chorchorus olitorius, the Awsun, one of the Solanaceæ, the Agbagba or Musa sapientum var: paradisiaca, the Yanrin or Lactuca sp, the Tete Aramanthus sp, the Ebolo or Gynura sp, the Odu (?), the Ajefawu (?), the Ebure or

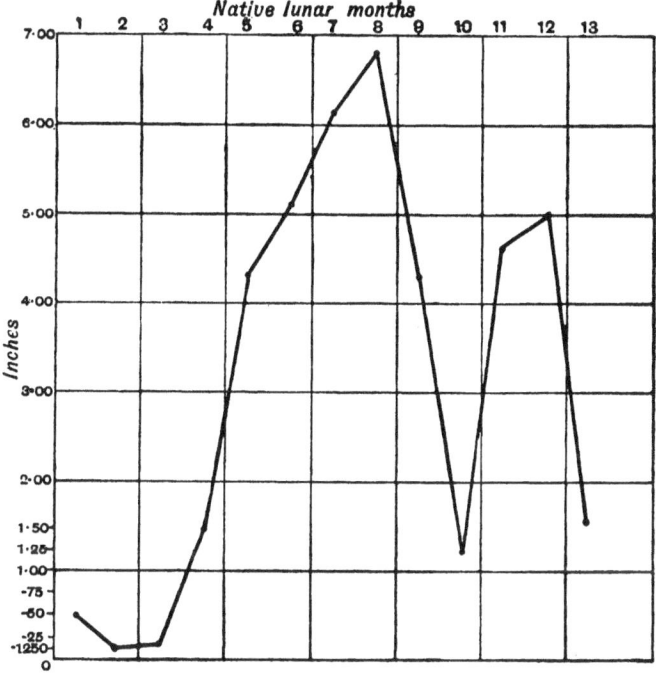

Gynura cernua, the Yangobi (?), the Ishapa or Hibiscus sp, the Ila or Hibiscus esculentus, the Awin or the Dialium guineensis and the Igba or the Parkia filicoidea.

The end of the rainy season and the beginning of the dry (about November) forms a kind of season by itself and is called Odun (year). The farmers go on weeding their farms to give the crops of their second harvest a chance. It is about the end of this season that babies of parents married in the spring are born. Before the long grass becomes dry and brittle they cut and stack it for re-roofing their houses.

The Dry Season.

The dry season is divided into two sections of two months each. White mists [1] cover the land, it is very hot during the day, and the temperature during the night falls as low as 52°, which we regard much as you at home look upon your freezing point. Bosman considered this great change of temperature as the cause of much of the sickness on the coast: "The unwholesomeness of this coast," he says, "in my opinion, seems chiefly owing to the heat of the day and coolness of the night, which sudden change I am induced to believe occasions several effects in our bodies, especially in those not accustomed to bear more heat than cold, by too hastily throwing off their clothes to cool too fast." Then Barbot tells us that "the air tho' not so cold is much thinner and more piercing than in England, and corrodes iron much faster." The cold wind blowing from the East is called the Harmattan by us and Oye by the natives, who liken it to a giant who lives in a cavern somewhere to the North of Ilorin, or then in the mountain Igebeti where the Devil rules supreme.

[1] It is possible that the ideas surrounding "Obatala" have been connected with this whiteness in the heavens, which commences as soon as the rains are over in November and December.

The farmers now gather their second harvest of corn, and that of beans and guinea-corn. They clear land for their next season's crops, and burn the drying bush they have already felled.

They now enjoy eating crickets, and the fruits of the Idofin tree and Ketemfe are added to their vegetable bill of fare. The leaves of the Ketemfe are called Ewe iran, and they are used also for roofing their houses.

This is their fishing season, when traps are placed at the mouths of all small streams.

Part II.

This dry season (Erun) continues for the next two months, but during the latter part of the second month rumbling thunder is heard, and small rains fall. The farmer goes on preparing the ground, and starts planting yams. They still eat crickets, and make good use of the semi-wild products already mentioned. Fishing of course goes on, but the long grass having been burnt and the fresh herbage making its appearance, this part of the dry season is the hunter's ideal time.

It is now perhaps time to consider the so-called fourteen months of the ancient Yoruba year. We have already pointed out the confusion in some observers' minds concerning the four days of the Yoruba week, which some say is composed of four days, and some of five. This same mystification recurs in the number of days said to complete one of

CALENDAR 1910

ANCIENT YORUBA YEAR OF 14 NATIVE MONTHS OR 224 DAYS

English											Yoruba
Saturday ...	Jan. 1	29	26	26	23	21	18	16	13	10	8	5	3	Obatala
Sunday ...	2	30	27	27	24	22	19	17	14	11	9	6	4	Ifa, Awu, or Eshu
Monday ...	3	31 Feb. 1	28 Mar. 1	**28**	25	23	20	**18**	15	12	10	**7**	5	**Odudua** or Ogun
Tuesday ...	4	1	1	29	26	24	21	19	16	13	11	8	6	Jakuta
Wednesday...	5	2	2	30	27	25	22	20	17	14	12	9	7	Obatala
Thursday ...	6	3	3	31 April 1	28	26	23	21	18	15	13	10	8	Ifa, Awu, or Eshu
Friday ...	7	4	4	1	**29**	27	24	22	**19**	16	14	11	9	**Odudua** or Ogun
Saturday ...	8	5	5	2	30 May 1	28	25	23	20	17	15	12	10	Jakuta
Sunday ...	9	6	6	3	1	29	26	24	21	18	16	13	11	Obatala
Monday ...	10	7	7	4	2	30	27	25	22	19	17	14	12	Ifa, Awu, or Eshu
Tuesday ...	11	8	8	5	3	31 June 1	28	26	23	**20**	18	15	13	**Odudua** or Ogun
Wednesday...	12	9	9	6	4	1	29	27	24	21	19	16	14	Jakuta

Day															Deity
Thursday ...	13	10	7	5	*2*	*30* *July*	*28*	*25*	*22*	*20*	17	15			Obatala
Friday ...	14	11	8	6	*3*	*1*	*29*	*26*	*23*	*21*	18	16			Ifa, Awu, or Eshu
Saturday ...	15	12	9	7	*4*	**2**	*30*	*27*	*24*	**22**	19	17			**Odudua** or Ogun
Sunday ...	16	13	10	8	*5*	*3*	*31* *Aug.*	*28*	*25*	*23*	20	18			Jakuta
Monday ...	17	14	11	9	*6*	*4*	*1*	*29*	*26*	*24*	21	19			Obatala
Tuesday ...	18	15	12	10	*7*	*5*	*2*	*30*	*27*	*25*	22	20			Ifa, Awu, or Eshu
Wednesday...	19	16	**13**	11	*8*	*6*	**3**	*31* *Sept.*	*28*	*26*	23	21			**Odudua** or Ogun
Thursday ...	20	17	14	12	*9*	*7*	*4*	*1*	*29*	*27*	24	22			Jakuta
Friday ...	21	18	15	13	*10*	*8*	*5*	*2*	*30* *Oct.*	*28*	25	23			Obatala
Saturday ...	22	19	16	14	*11*	*9*	*6*	*3*	*1*	*29*	26	24			Ifa, Awu, or Eshu
Sunday ...	23	20	17	**15**	*12*	*10*	*7*	**4**	*2*	*30*	27	25			**Odudua** or Ogun
Monday ...	24	21	18	16	*13*	*11*	*8*	*5*	*3*	*31* *Nov.*	28	26			Jakuta
Tuesday ...	25	22	19	17	*14*	*12*	*9*	*6*	*4*	*1*	29	27			Obatala
Wednesday...	26	23	20	18	*15*	*13*	*10*	*7*	*5*	*2*	30	28			Ifa, Awu, or Eshu
Thursday ...	27	24	21	19	**16**	*14*	*11*	*8*	**6**	*3*	Dec. 1	29			**Odudua** or Ogun
Friday ...	28	25	22	20	*17*	*15*	*12*	*9*	*7*	*4*	2	30			Jakuta
Saturday ...	—	—	—	—	—	—	—	—	—	—	—	31 Jan. 1911			Obatala
Sunday ...	—	—	—	—	—	—	—	—	—	—	—	1			Ifa, Awu, or Eshu

The figures in Italics denote the ancient Yoruba year, which commenced on the 28th March and ended on the 6th November.

their months. Some say that there are sixteen, and others seventeen, days in a native month. The natives, as we have already explained, rest on the fifth day, that is to say, having counted four days, they really rest on the first day of the next week, counting that day as one. So in their next great division of time they say that they rest on the seventeenth day, which is a great market day, and this is, of course, the first day of what is their second so-called month. Fourteen of these months completed the ancient Yoruba so-called year. In other words, the ancients only valued the rain season. It was the first rumble of thunder that recalled the fisherman and hunter to their huts, and caused them to commence to count the days. They thought the father in heaven had set his Forger Ogun to work to make his thunderbolts so that he might carry on his war to secure wives.

The ancient Yoruba then counted four weeks of four days, and on the seventeenth day put one cowry in a calabash or gourd, and when he had counted fourteen of these he knew it was nearing the time when his pregnant wife should bear him a child. That is to say, the eighth month which he feared for his wife's sake was now ended. This was the all-important part of the year to him, the rest of the time after the birth of his child he occupied in fishing and hunting. Thus to him the year was composed of $4 \times 4 \times 14$, or 224 days. And thus we hear of the Yoruba speaking of his having fourteen months in his year, and the traveller, concluding that he is referring to lunar months, is puzzled. And in many localities we still find that it is only during the rain season that the worship of *local* Orishas takes place. In asking natives for the names of the months of the lunar year seven or eight Orishas' names only have at times been given to me. This seems to me to show that the Ifa lunar calendar system is of a later date, which has not even yet, in many parts, become general.

We will now return to our lunar calendar.

The Rain Season.

The season of rain may be divided into two parts separated one from the other by a little dry season. The first section is composed of five lunar months of rain, the latter of two lunar months, one nearly dry month intervening.

The first two months of this section of the rains is called Asheroh ojo. It is the tornado season when thunder, lightning, wind and rain, and Jakuta, the stone-thrower, all do their best to frighten the timid into a proper consideration of their powers. And I think no one of us who has experienced some of these great storms will dare to say that on some occasion or other a very loud clap of thunder has not made him jump, as the saying goes. I remember once at a place called Musuku on the Kongo river a man and his wife and child were all struck senseless by thunder, as they were not struck by lightning. Luckily, I have never experienced any accident of this terrible nature, but I have been caught in the bush by "Zaci and his twenty-four dogs," as they call thunder and lightning in the Kongo, and wished myself well out of it.

While on this subject I think we may all congratulate ourselves on not having been in Axim in the year 1693 or 1694, when, Bosman says, "the thunder broke all the drinking glasses of the Factor's chamber, and raised up his child with the bed under it, both which it threw some feet distant, without the least hurt done. What do you think, Sir? Was it possible for a stone to do this? I believe not." I think we are all wise enough to-day to agree with Bosman, but the stone-thrower, Jakuta, has a good deal to answer for in Yorubaland.

At the beginning of this season the farmer plants his first crop of corn and groundnuts, and later Bara, Igba, and Agbe, or gourds used by them for all manner of household purposes. Mushrooms are now added to his bill of fare. This is the ancient season of marriage.

The next two months compose the season when the rainfall reaches its maximum. The farmer weeds and keeps his farm as tidy as he can, but everything grows apace, and he has to work hard if he wishes to reap a fair harvest. He is rewarded towards the end of the second month by being able to eat new corn. His main crop, however, is left standing until it is quite dry, which is not until the little dry season sets in, in the next season. He gathers the fruit of the Emi ori or Shea butter tree, and mushrooms are still to be found.

This subdivision of the rain season is called Aga,

probably because the corn has grown tall during the last month. The Yoruba have a saying that the woman who is married in the month of Aga will eat pounded corn.

The Awori season is composed of one month of rain and the little dry season. The farmer digs up his first crop of yams, and gathers in his corn and ground nuts and gourds. Before the rains have stopped he has sown the seed for a second crop of corn, beans, ground nuts, and guinea-corn and he also now sows cotton.

This is said to be a marriage season also, but it is evidently a time of harvest.

The next two months are called the Arokuro season, and, like the first two months of the rains, they are tornado months. Farmers fell the bush for next year's farms, and keep on weeding.

CHAPTER XIV

OKE, OKO, AJESHALUGA, AND FARMING.

Farmland and Farmers, and the Orishas Oke, Oko and Ajeshaluga.

YORUBALAND may be divided into three great zones, one of very little use to the farmer as farmland, but of service to him as the zone that in the olden days provided him with salt, *i.e.* the Mangrove belt. Here the seaside inhabitant used to cut down the salt bush and manufacture salt, which he sent with smoked fish into the interior. and exchanged for farm produce. Here also oyster shells were burnt and lime made, but this does not appear to have been used by the farmers, and I think we may conclude that the industry was acquired from the early white settlers. The native farmers have long known that leguminous crops nourish the land, but they have not yet learnt the use of lime as a manure, although it is perhaps the manure most needed in this country.

The next zone as you travel inland is composed of evergreen tropical forests and mixed forests, in which we find the excellent Egba farmers.

The third zone is that which is called the dry open

forest, where the rainfall is from thirty to forty-five inches per annum. For a full description of these zones I must refer you to the Conservator of Forests' Report on the Forest Administration of Southern Nigeria for 1906.

The Yoruba call the forest land Igbo, the mixed forest Odan, and the open grassland Pappa.

Forest land is generally felled during the latter rains and the dry season.

In the open grass country the grass is burnt in the dry season, and the land cultivated for three or four years, and then allowed to lie fallow for some years, but the forest land will stand from five to seven years' crops, and even then water yams and plantains may be grown on it. This land is then allowed to lie fallow for two or three years, when it is again brought into use for two or three years: then it used to be allowed to lie fallow for twenty or thirty years. Farm land is known as Oko, and fallow as Ashale.

The farmer also knows a great deal more about soils than is generally credited to him. He prefers, naturally enough, the good loamy forest land which he calls Ebole, a stony loam he names Ebole olokuta, the sandy loam Ilero: then he talks of red and black soils as Ilepa and Iledu. Clay he terms Amo, and it is of a yellow colour, the white clay he calls Amofunfun, and that which is mixed with sand and cracks in the dry season is known by the name Tara. Sand is called Yanrin.

It will be readily understood that in this study of the native farmer I am not attempting to write an up-to-date paper on the state of agriculture in Southern Nigeria. On the contrary I am purposely leaving out all mention of all our Agege and other advanced planters, of whom we are all so justly proud. I am, in fact, dealing only with the less favoured so-called pagan farmer in his capacity as a worshipper of certain Orishas.

The Egba farmer is a very pleasant and hospitable man to meet, as well as most interesting. One of these simple folk told me that when it was time to fell the bush to make a new farm he gave a present to his chief, and asked him to give him some people to help. On the day fixed for their coming he prepared food for them. They cut the bush, and ate and drank at his expense. He and his family then burnt the felled timber, and when the first rains came he sowed corn. For two or three years he planted corn and yams on this land, he also planted beans with the corn. He said Ebole land might be used for as many as ten or eleven years before it was exhausted. Ilero soil was good for corn and yams for two or three years.

If the land belongs to the farmer the produce is his own, but if he has been allowed to farm it by the owner he has to give him a part of the product.

Before planting they generally offered some sacrifice to their departed parents, and asked them to see that their crops were successful. He said he knew a man who, to get good beans, used to mix a powder with his seed.

When yams begin to sprout, and the first leaves

XIV OKE, OKO, AJESHALUGA, AND FARMING

begin to appear, women are not allowed to go on the yam fields. A man at Ilaro, that he knew, was very strict on this point, and prohibited all women from walking through the fields, lest any with menses should go, and so spoil the yam crop. He also told me that the farmer's Orishas were Oke, Oko and Ajeshaluga.

Agbolo's son, a great hunter and farmer, told me that the farmers near Olokemeji had a society for mutual help, called Aro or Owe. This was composed of four great officers, Ashipa, Obawunju, Oluri and Ekesin, and that these four were helped by a kind of Council of twelve, composed of six Iwarefa and six Egbe Iwarefa. It was a semi-religious society, and Ashipa, when the rains failed, about April, was asked to offer a sacrifice to Oke. They made a little mound of earth, and planted bananas round it. They then killed a cock, and took four kola nuts and placed them on the mound. They next went home, and cooked some yams, and pounded them into a kind of pudding. This they carried to the mound, and taking the cock whose blood had all soaked into the earth, they cooked it and ate it with the yams. They also poured rum or gin or palm wine on the mound. Then, as they danced and prayed, the rain came. At the time of the new yams they sacrificed to Oko, who was their Orisha of harvest. And at the end of the year, when all their crops were stored, they assembled in Ashipa's house, and he sacrificed to the Orisha of wealth, Shaluga or Ajeshaluga. I visited the Ashipa, and he confirmed this. I then asked him if these three were the only Orishas the farmers worshipped, and he said "Yes." I mentioned that I had been informed that Yemoja had thirteen children. "Yes." I continued, "I can account for seven— Olokun and Olosa, the Orishas of the fishermen ; Ogun and Oshowsi, the Orishas of the hunters ; Oke, Oko [1] and Shaluga, the farmer's Orishas ; could he tell me anything about the others?" "Yes, Shango, Oshun, Oba and Oya were marriage Orishas, and Shankpana was the Orisha of sickness, and Dada the Orisha of babies and things created." He was kind enough to refer me to one Odedaino, who, he said, could tell me all about marriage.

Just as the farm Orishas, Oke and Oko, have become associated with the marriage Orishas Shango and Oshun, so the marriage Orisha Oya, one of the wives of Shango, cannot well be separated from the farmers' Orisha of wealth and colour, Ajeshaluga. In fact, the literal meaning of the word Ya is to pluck Indian corn. These Orishas will finally fall into their places, in accordance with the seasons they appear to influence. The beginning of the rain, or Ashero ojo season, is the old marriage season, thus Shango, the great marriage Orisha, and Oke, the rain Orisha, clearly lead the way. Then we have the marriage Orisha, Oshun, and the harvest Orisha Oko ruling the following season of two months called Aga, leaving us with Oya and Ajeshaluga as the gatherer and wealth maker ruling the season of harvest of dry corn, and of all fruit.

[1] A minor Orisha is called Agbarigbo, who is said to be a guardian at the gate or entrance on the way to the farm.

I mention this now, as I wish to be free to describe the Orishas separately and independently of the seasons under the heading of farmer or marriage.

Ajeshaluga

Ajeshaluga, or Shaluga, is a very interesting Orisha, and it is easy to see why he is the farmers' deity, for they were possibly the first to accumulate wealth. The word Ajé is translated "money"; Aje means trial by water, and Ajeh is a witch. (No doubt the people envying the wealthy declared them to be witches, and put them to trial by water. In the Congo even the so-called "King," while he might own a large house, had to reside in a small one, so as not to cause the envy of his people. This, incidentally, may be one of the reasons why the natives of Africa have never advanced beyond a certain stage of civilisation.) Shalu is to recur, and ga is to be tall, high : gàn is to despise.

The word seems to convey the idea of a stretching out to add money to money. Naturally he presides over money transactions, and Bishop Crowther quotes a proverb "Ajé Shalua, ofi eni iwaju sile she eni ehin ni pele, ori ki awran ki aw tan : Ajé often passes by the first caravan, as it comes to the market, and loads the last with blessings" (*i.e.* the race is not always to the swift).

The prevailing colour in the market where wealth is acquired is indigo blue, and in this way perhaps Aje Shaluga has been and is the patron of colour. The large cowry is his emblem. The Yoruba for cowry is Owo, which also means money, wealth, trade, craft. Weight is evidently also connected with wealth, as a great number of cowries weigh a good deal, in fact the word used for weight, heaviness, importance is Wuwo, the act of increasing cowries.

CHAPTER XV

ODUS OF IFA

The Ifa Priests and Odus

JUST as it is necessary to know something of the seasons before understanding the place the farm Orishas take in the philosophy of the Yoruba, so before touching on marriage we must pause and consider the priests of Ifa, and their system of divination.

The sixteen snails of Yemuhu (or Odudua), Oja told me, became the head of Eleda, and apparently in the worship of Ifa sixteen (plus one) palm kernels, or Odus, take their place. The Yoruba word for a snail is Igbin, and the verb Gbin is to breathe with difficulty, so that Igbin means literally that which breathes with difficulty. Igba, you will remember, is the calabash cut in two representing heaven and earth, within which Obatala and Odudua were enclosed. I quote later on a native legend from *Historical Notes of the Yoruba People* by Mr. George, where the breaking of Igba causes famine. Igba also means the number 200, and is said to be the calabash in which the 201 Odus of Ifa are kept.

Awnomila is the Bini for Orunmila, another name for Ifa, and amongst those people it is the name of a small basin wrapped in cloth containing the Iviawnomila, or sixteen sacred palm nuts of Ifa.

Bishop Johnson says: " He (Ifa) is represented chiefly by sixteen palm nuts, each having from four to ten, or more, eyelets on them. Behind each one of these representative nuts are sixteen subordinate divinities. Each one of the whole lot is termed an Odu, which means a chief, a head. This makes the number of Odus altogether 256. Besides these there are sixteen other Odus connected with each of the 256, and this makes the whole number of Odus 4,096. Some increase this large number still by a further addition of sixteen to each of the last number of Odus, but the sixteen principal ones are those more frequently in requisition.

" There is a series of traditional stories, each of which is called a road and is connected with a particular Odu. Each Odu is supposed to have 1,680 of these stories connected with it."

Bishop Phillips has collected about 105 of these and given them to us in his little Yoruba book called *Ifa*.

Ellis (pages 59–60 the *Yoruba-speaking Peoples*) says : " For the consultation of Ifa a whitened board is employed, exactly similar to those used by children in Moslem Schools in lieu of slates, about two feet long and eight or nine inches broad, on which are marked sixteen figures. These figures are called ' mothers.' The sixteen palm nuts are held loosely in the right hand, and thrown through the half closed fingers into the left hand. If one nut remains in the right hand, two marks are made, thus—11, and if two remain one mark—1. This process is repeated eight times, and the marks are made in succession in two columns of four each. In this way are formed the sixteen mothers, one of which is declared by the Babalawo to represent the enquirer;[1] and from the order in which the others are produced he deduces certain results."

Ellis then gives the sixteen " mothers."

I obtained the order of the Odus from Oliyitan, an Ifa priest, and to make sure that the order was correct so far as he was concerned, I asked him to give me the order again about three months afterwards. As it was exactly the same I have adopted this as correct.

It may therefore be of interest to give Bishop Johnson's, Bishop Phillips', Colonel Ellis' and my list side by side to see how far they agree.

Ellis'.	*Johnson's.*	*Phillips'.*	*The Writer's.*
...	Ogbe	Ogbe	Ogbe
Yekuru	Oyekun	Oyeku	Oyeku
...	Iwori	Iwori	Iwori
Di	Edi	Odi	Odi
Loshu	Urosi	Iroshu	Iroshun
...	Owaran	Owourin	Owourin
...	Bara	Obara	Obara
...	Okaran	Okauran	Okouron
Kuda	Ogunda	Oguda	Oguda

[1] There are 16 plus 1 nuts, and as far as my information goes the 17th is the enquirer.

Ellis'.	Johnson's.	Phillip's.	The Writer's.
Sa	Osa	Osa	Osa
Ka	Eka	Ika	Ika
Durapin	Oturupon	Oturupon	Oturupon
Ture	Eture	Otura	Otura
Leti	Erete	Irete	Irete
Shi	Ose	Oshe	Oshe
Fu	Ofu	Ofu	Ofu

Ellis mentions also the following Akala, Abila, Orun, Ode, Buru. Bishop Phillips, in addition to the above, gives—Ate, Tutu, Oka, Adoka, Egutan Oriko, Egu, Sete, Dawo, Osutele, and Itegu.

On page 215 of *At the Back of the Black Man's Mind* I give as one of the chalk marks renewed on the first day of the week in front of the sacred groves, the following :

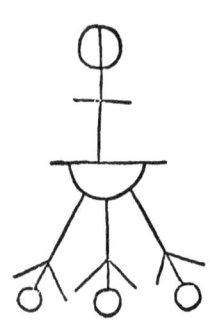

I will now give you the reading of this figure.

Ifa is known by the name Owa, the being whose advent filled men with joy. He is also Orunmila, or Heaven and the wise Reconciler. In this figure the sun is called Baba ye Omo, another name for Ifa, meaning " Father."

This is Ifa in his character as the heavenly revealer, the Sun, but he is also the propagator, and this is where secrecy and darkness come in, so there is a line drawn dividing the light side of his character from that which is dark and secret. As I have pointed out, he is here represented by Eshu, which is the next figure, *i.e.* that of the new moon; and this is called Odu or Edu, that which is black, or, as they say, the "one that troubles have made black." I have already pointed out that Odu=Oshu, the moon; Edu thus is another form of Eshu, the devil, or Ifa, as procreator. Odu or Eshu is in the place of the Bashorun, as President of the Council, and as he is helped by three officers so Odu is helped by the three symbols representing the three stars. Their names are given as—

Ogbe Meji, the one that succours.
Oyeku ,, the one that heralds.
Iwori ,, the one that sets.

Representing the treasurer, the messenger, and the arbitrator.

As we have noted, there is always a questioner who asks the Diviners something. In this case it is the 17th Odu, or the one that stands aside, and its name is Odin or Edi. The verb Di=Da to make or create. Thus we can conclude that the questioner asks, "What about Creation?" Taking the order as given to me by the Babalawo the answer is:

Iroshun	=	filtration	} water	
Owourin	=	that which drizzles		
Obara	=	that which bears the oil seed Egusi	} earth	
Okoron	=	the dry bed of a river		
Oguda	=	that which pounds and creates	} heat marriage rain	
Osa	=	that which dries and evaporates		
Ika	=	he who reaps, harvest	} 1st harvest	{ in making of man "Conception"
Oturupon	=	he who gathers		

Otura Irete	{ translated to me as ease, happiness, hope, when there is no anxiety about food, a time of fruitfulness	{ in the making of man, the time when the woman shows signs of pregnancy and she is happy and hopeful
Oshe Ofu	= that which shall be = emission	{ to appear in the wrong month without being expected } pain, suffering, travail

Taking these Odus in the order thus given to me, and remembering the order of the seasons, there can be no doubt that they tell us of the order of propagation; neither can one doubt from the literal translations given that the categories and their order which I discovered to be at the back of the Black man's mind in the Congo are also at the back of the mind of the Yoruba Babalawo. But this will be more plainly seen when I have finished describing the parts that the offspring of Yemoja fill in the "Ogboni" of the Orishas.

According to Bishop Johnson in his "Yoruba Heathenism," there are three grades of Babalawo (see page 251 *At the Back of the Black Man's Mind*), but Ifa's Ogboni is composed of the following priests:

Babalawo, Olowo, Odofin, Asawo.
Ajigbona and assistant } who offer human sacrifice.
Awaro ,, ,,
Aro ,, ,,
Asarepawo ,, ,,
Apetebi or Ayawo and assistant.

N.B. Bishop Johnson, in *Yoruba Heathenism*, tells us the priestess called Apetebi, Esu or Ayawo, who may in reality be the wife of a priest or of anyone for whom a sacrifice is to be offered, is regarded as the wife of Orunmila or Ifa.

I have not discovered the name of the sixth and his assistant.

The place these priests take in marriage and birth ceremonies will shortly be shown under the chapter headed " Marriage." We have had a "flood" story, and noted the part played by Ifa in making the world fit again for human habitation. In the following extracts from Mr. George's story of the breaking of Igba at Ife, Ifa as Orunmila plays a notable part in the fall of man, his punishment by famine, and his salvation.

As Mr. George says, all Ifa's sayings generally open with some sort of aphoristic verse which invariably explains the whole object of the piece. Thus, the first verse tells how all the world met in the King's courtyard to discuss the cause of the breaking of the world-renowned Igba, or calabash, of Ife.

1. They called Awlawta to come and put it together again, but he could not.
2. Beni ado from Ife } were called.
3. Owo from Etu
4. Ogun also is sent for ; which means that war was declared over this breakage.

But none of them could put the calabash together again.

People farmed and waited for the rain, but none came. Then hunger came, and man and beast mourned for their dead.

5. The Obalufon from Iyinde.
6. Laberinjo from Ido.
7. Jigure from Otun Moba.
8. Esegba, an Egba.

9. Asadu from Ijesa.
10. Akoda from Ife.
11. Aseda Araba (the law-giving cotton tree), their father.
All these could not put the calabash together again.
Then the pigeon weakens in the Eselu bush.
The snail does the like in the bamboo, etc.
They could not put the calabash together again.
They call
12. Olumo from Imori.
13. Ogun of Alara.
14. Ogbon of Ijero.
15. Odudugbundu of Eshemaiva, the Awbawle bogun Baba wow Ketu Er, the father devil who lived in Ketu.
But all these could do nothing.

To continue, in verse 3 the people call in

1. Akonilogbon, and
2. Afonahanni, and ask their assistance.
They advised them to call in
3. Ototo Enia, the truthful one. They asked him to call Olofin. He refused. But the people reminded him "that from the beginning at the creation of the world this duty of trumpeter to the man from heaven was specially laid on him. Then he blew his trumpet, and the elephant went quickly to the Eselu bush, the wild ox to Elugu apako, the bird Kekeke flies to the ale plant, the rat runs to its hole, the beans to the brook, the dog to the land of meditation, the sheep to the country of stupidity, all beasts go to beastland, beings go to the land of beings." In fact, as when Oro is sounded all non-members of the Society fly to their homes.

1. And Ajalaiye, he who strives with earthly affairs,
2. And Ajalorun, he who strives with heavenly affairs.
3. Ajirilogbon, he who strives with matters concerning sight and wisdom.

The people confess their filth, and pray that he should patch the broken calabash, and Ajirilogbon tells them to go and find the leaf of a tree called Ewe-Alashuwalu (which is said to be capable of remodelling a man's evil character). They cannot find it. He then takes it out of the bag of Egede (the bag of deep mystery), and mends the broken Igba of Ife, and rain falls, and so heals all the people, and stops the calamity from causing further harm.

And in this way we find that Ifa and his priests are not only concerned with marriage, but also with the rains and the sin that prevents them falling in due season.

This story of the breaking of the calabash and the calling of all these worthies to patch it reminds one of the story of Humpty Dumpty, and how all the king's courtiers and all the king's men could not put Humpty Dumpty together again.

With this short account of Ifa, his priests and their Odus, we will close this note and proceed to describe the marriage Orishas.

CHAPTER XVI

SHANGO—OYA—OBA—OSHUN

Marriage

IN *African Life and Customs* (page 22) that remarkable African author, Dr. E. W. Blyden, speaking of Jamaica, says: "Now it is into this region of the globe so hostile to the most vigorous European life that Anglo-Saxon incuriousness has introduced the marriage laws of Europe, with the result that during the last three hundred years very few Europeans, if any, born in those islands have achieved anything like an international reputation. And why? Their mothers have not observed the regulation period of rest and reserve which African mothers enjoy. They were tired when the children were born, and the children have suffered the same inability. There have been exceptional cases of noted men born in the West Indies sufficiently distinguished to be honoured by their sovereign with the Companionship of the Bath and with Knighthood, but these were men of mixed blood, who were born practically under polygamic conditions, whose mothers enjoyed the necessary period of rest."

Oke and Oko as farm Orishas are worshipped in the outer districts without any of these phallic ceremonies. But at the yearly festival at Ibadan and Abeokuta these priest daughters exist. It is still considered a great honour to the family to get one of their daughters elected to the office, which is hereditary in certain families; and most of the members of the family, even the husband, feel honoured by contributing to the fund to cover the expense incurred.

The rites connected with Oke and Oko are evidently intended, as Dr. Frazer has pointed out in his book, "Adonis, Attis, Osiris," to ensure the fruitfulness of the ground and the increase of man and beast on the principle of homœopathic magic.

In an interesting discussion in the *African Mail* on the marriage question in Africa, a correspondent, signing himself "A Negro Lover of Consistency," poured out the vials of his wrath on the head of the departed Col. Ellis, and spoke of the passage quoted above and such stories about the African as "spurious bosh." I am not quite prepared to credit

---

On the same god F. S., in the *Nigerian Chronicle* of the 26th of March, says :—

"Orisha Oko's name was ' Kubiya.' His first occupation was to catch wild guinea fowls and sell them. He afterwards became a physician, and was such an extraordinary man that his powers were considered supernatural. He resided in a village where all men came to him, for he was a very skilful medical man and diviner. He was called Orisa-Oko ['Village god'] because he lived in a village."

Here Orisha Oko was originally a trapper and guinea fowl seller and ultimately a physician.

this "Lover of Consistency" with a proper motive in thus attacking a man no longer able to defend himself, whom he believed to be a kind of enemy of his race, but I can pity him as the product of a spurious form of Christianity which thinks that by hiding the past, his race is, in some magical way, benefited. He is like that son full of false pride who is ready to inherit the wealth and position his father has left him, but is ashamed of his humble origin. Great teachers not only have great ideals to which they lead the minds of their disciples, but they also know all about the past, and so are able to warn them of the pitfalls they must try to shun. The best way to learn how to appreciate the beauties of a purely spiritual religion is by trying to grasp all the beauties in a natural one. The spiritual simply uplifts and fulfils the natural.

When these two great festivals were first instituted, it must be remembered, wars between village and village, town and town, were the rule, but upon these days all united, and, under the protection of these Orishas, met on more or less an equal footing. It reminds one of the description given by an old Arabist writer of the Hajj:—"It (the festival) formed the rendezvous of ancient Arabian life. Here came under the protection of God the tribes and clans which at other times lived apart, and only knew peace and security within their own frontiers. Here affairs between states or tribes were transacted and adjusted. Of course lively proceedings and dealings went on between individuals, for this was the single opportunity when men could move freely in and out among one another without fear. Here slaves are bought or redeemed, acquaintances made and courtships arranged between men and women of different tribes, which could otherwise never be carried on." The difficulty of obtaining wives in small villages without incest is one of the possible causes of the founding of these farm festivals. We must all remember the difficulty of the sons of Benjamin. 'Then the elders of the congregation said, " How shall we do for wives for them that remain, seeing that the women are destroyed out of Benjamin ?"

"'And they said, " There must be an inheritance for them that be escaped of Bejamin, that a tribe be not destroyed out of Israel."

"'Howbeit we may not give them wives of our daughters : for the children of Israel have sworn, saying, "Cursed be he who giveth a wife to Benjamin."

"'Then they said, "Behold there is a feast of the Lord in Shiloh yearly in a place which is on the north side of Bethel, on the east side of the high way that goeth up from Bethel to Shechem, and on the south of Lebonah."

"'Therefore they commanded the children of Benjamin, saying "Go and lie in wait in the vineyards; and see, and behold, if the daughters of Shiloh come out to dance in dances, then come out of the vineyards, and catch you every man his wife of the daughters of Shiloh, and go to the land of Benjamin."

"'And the children of Benjamin did so. In those days there was no king in Israel: every man did that which was right in his own eyes.'"

However pure and good the intention of the founders of these feasts may have been at the time of their inauguration, it is certain that in course of ages the beauty of the original idea was lost and they possibly became the orgiastic festivals in this part of Africa that we know they became in Greece and Italy in days gone by. And now that peace reigns here and roads and railways are opening the country, native public opinion is fast siding against all that is evil in these customs, and they are once again assuming their true aspect in the form of "prayers for rain in due season," harvest thanksgivings, and agricultural shows.

The Orisha Oke may well be called the titular goddess of Ibadan. When the chiefs of that place were asked what animal or sign they would like as an emblem to figure on the medals to be given away at their agricultural show, they unanimously selected Oke. They had the photograph of a fine looking woman taken, her breasts exposed, and her arms raised towards heaven, as if to welcome her children. A picture of fruitfulness. She is the hill Orisha, connected with fire. Her festival used to be held when the land was at its driest and rain was most required to quench its thirst. She would appear to a man in a dream and tell him

SHANGO—OYA—OBA—OSHUN

to go to the Bale and ask him to fix a day for the feast. Perhaps the Bale would take no notice, and then she would visit another man in a dream and ask him to go. If the Bale hesitated she threatened to send fire down from heaven to burn his house and cause him a great loss. She sometimes demanded a man as a sacrifice, sometimes 200 pigeons, sometimes a bullock or a sheep. Notice would be sent round to all the villages and the day stated. Everyone had to be in the town the day before the date fixed. Anyone coming into the town on the day of the festival would be robbed of all he might be bringing with him. No trade was done, and the Bale threw money away among the crowds of people, who, in bands of males and bands of females of different ranks and ages, paraded the town, throwing open their cloths as they met as if to invite copulation. Wives told their husbands that they were going to play and they allowed them to go, and the wives picked out the men they fancied and cohabited with them. Bands of women passing down the streets sang :—

    Septeni nascimur, utinam et ipsa septem pariam :
    Ido niger est, uterus penitus ruber,
    Uterus duobus milibus concharum constat, sed
      penis quindecim tantum conchis.
    Eum cui penis est penem condere oportet, quod
      uterum medio in corpore habeo.
    Foris est mater olearii
    Foris est pater olearii
    Filius natu maximus olearii

Sub porticu dormit.
Tollo pannum et insero :
" Kerekere " sonit, et penem quaerere os uteri sentio.

At the foot of the two hills from which Olokemeji takes its name there is an altar to Oke, and there is a cavern in the rocks at Abeokuta in which Oke is said to be worshipped. The Egba say that if they were defeated in war they could retire into this cave and it would hermetically seal itself up until the danger were passed.

The Orisha Oko, or harvest god, whose emblem is an iron rod and who has the title of "eni duru," or the erect person, is more in evidence at Abeokuta than elsewhere. His festival is held about August. His bride daughters, like the daughters of kings, may cohabit with whom they please. These Iyawo Orisha have a red and white mark on their foreheads. The office is hereditary, but when the mother dies Ifa is consulted as to which of her daughters is to take her place. The family collects from £40 to £50 to cover the expenses of the initiation ceremony. They make a shed in the bush and keep the girl there for three months. She is given what she fancies, and feasting goes on all the time. She is washed every day, and the marks are renewed by a male and a female attendant, called respectively. " Baba losha and Iya losha." After three months they wash her and paint her head, arms and feet red and white. The people then sing and dance around her and prostrate themselves before her for seven days. She is now called Olu Orisha Oko.

Sacred Cave at Abeokuta.

From the fact that these farm Orishas only become phallic in the great centres of population, I am inclined to think that this phallic worship is a development that only came about when people began to live in large towns, where great feasts were held.

Agbolo had referred me to one Odedaino as an expert on the marriage question, so to him I went for enlightenment on this burning topic. He said they knew a girl was ready for marriage, as then she first had her menses (aseh). Girls were given in marriage sometimes as babies. Two families wished to be drawn together, and they agreed that their children should intermarry. A boy or a man took a fancy to a child and asked the parents through his parents for their child in marriage. The first thing the father of the girl did was to consult Ifa. Ifa's priest (Babalawo) having been called in, he proceeded to divine as explained in the chapter on Ifa. Then if "Eji ogbe" turns up, the engagement may take place; but if Osa or Ofu turn up, the Orisha not being in its favour, the application is not accepted. If the Orisha is propitious, the boy presents the parents with nine yams and 100 heads of corn,[1] and repeats this offering yearly. He also makes a sacrifice to Ifa. At the proper time the boy presents himself before the parents of the girl and says, "Now she is ready, give her to me."

The parents again consult Ifa, who may put off the marriage for a year.

In the olden days marriages took place at the

[1] This present appears to vary in different districts.

beginning of the rains, but as there was very little food in the house at that season the time was changed to the time of the harvest of the new yams, which was a time of great rejoicing (Orisha Oko), and the second planting season. When the parents have given their consent, and the young man has come to claim his bride, he must sacrifice to his Orisha: and on the day of his marriage he must sacrifice to his bride's Orisha. The parents give their daughter a white handkerchief and take her to the bridegroom's house. She is dressed in costly clothes, beautiful beads around her neck and waist, silver chains around her neck, and rings on her fingers. As she is supposed to be a maiden, plenty of rum and kola is presented. On the third day the wife goes back to her parents and takes the white handkerchief with her. If it has blood on it all is well, but, if not, she is asked to say who seduced her. The seducer has then to give damages to the would-be husband, who may refuse to acknowledge her as his wife. The chiefs on the husband's side settle the amount of damages. If, on the other hand, all is well, then they worship the Orisha called Ori (head) and the girl becomes the young man's wife. And if after a time she does not conceive, they give her medicine called "Idadure," and they ask the girl's Orisha to help them, and if this fails they then say it is the fault of the man, and they give him another girl so as to prove it. And if the latter does not conceive then they are sure that it is the man's fault. They next ask him to take medicine, and, after a certain time, if neither of the girls conceive, they take them away, and the man who eventually marries the girl pays back the dowry to the sterile would-be husband. From the time of marriage to the time of birth there are no Orisha ceremonies, but when the child is born they ask the priest to what Orisha they owe this good fortune, and when he tells them they sacrifice to it. Three days after the birth they call in the priest and ask him to name the child's "Ese entele" or footprints. The Babalawo consults Ifa, who, as the priest mentions an Orisha, shakes his head until that which is to become the guardian spirit of the child is mentioned. The child, as soon as it is able, fetches water for this Orisha and sacrifices to it on all great occasions during its life. If Obatala is the Orisha then the child must wear white and must not drink palm wine nor eat dog. The grand-parents as well as the parents on the safe delivery of their child each thank their separate Orishas. The priest gives the mother medicine for the preservation of the child. If it be a girl, a name is given to it on the seventh day, if a boy, on the ninth.

Except that it is never done in the dry season, and generally before the tenth year, there is no special time for circumcision of the boy, or the excision of the girl's clitoris, but the ceremony is performed when the child is in good health, and it is marked with its tribal marks on the same day.

Bosman in his description of the Kingdom of Benin, which is an offspring of the Yoruba, says: "Eight or fourteen days after the birth of their children, both male and females are circumcised, the former are thereby bereft of their prepuce and the latter of their clitoris, besides which they make small incisions all over the bodies of the infants, in a sort of regular manner expressing some figures thereby."

Bala Mimi, who accompanied Odedaino when this information was given to me, told me that the only marriage Orishas born of Yemoja were Shango and his wives Oya, Oba and Oshun, while Dada, Shango's brother, otherwise called Bayoni, was rather an Orisha of birth.

Ellis gives us a very good description of the Orisha Shango; he says: "He dwells in the clouds in an immense brazen palace, where he maintains a large retinue and a great number of horses." The Oni-Shango or priests of Shango in their chants always speak of Shango as hurling stones, and whenever a house is struck by lightning they rush in a body to pillage it and to find the stone, which, as they take it with them secretly, they always succeed in doing. A chant of the Oni-Shango very commonly heard is:— "Oh, Shango, thou art the master. Thou takest in thy hand thy fiery stones, to punish the guilty and satisfy thy anger." Everything that they strike is destroyed. Their fire eats up the forest, the trees are broken down, and all living creatures are slain, and the lay worshippers of Shango flock into the streets during a thunderstorm crying :—" Shango, Shango, great King. Shango is the Lord and Master. In the storms he hurls his fiery stones against his enemies, and their track gleams in the midst of the darkness." "May Shango's stone strike you," is a very common form of imprecation. He usually goes armed with a club called Oshe, made of the wood of the ayan tree, which is so hard that a proverb says:—" The ayan tree resists the axe."

His male followers are called Odushushango and the female Esin nla (the great horse).

I happened to meet an Odushushango, named Idowu, who gave me the following information. Jakuta is the name of Shango's day. Shango is the Alafin of Oyo's great Orisha and is sometimes called Oba Kuso, the king of Kuso, a hill near Oyo which is sacred to him.

Another name is Alada Ogun, the one who splits the mortar that Ogun is said to wear on his head. Ako aja abinrinja lese, the ako dog that walks as one about to fight. Aja jumoni koto kpanije, the one who frightens one before he kills and eats him. Olilu tun ilu re she, one who puts his town in order. Ebi ti ka waw ponyin shoro, the one who with his hands behind his back does him an injury. Akuwarapa abija kaka, the one who has fits and is extraordinarily strong.

His wife Oya[1] is she who runs on ahead when Shango goes out to fight, the strong tornado wind.

Oshun is the gathering darkness and Oba the wild clouds that meet. These two stay at home to keep house.

They sacrifice the cow, the sheep and the cock

---

[1] Oya is said to be the river spirit of the river Niger, and Bishop Crowther describes her as the wife of Thunder.

to Shango.[1] His sacred tree is the Ayan from which his staff is made. His ewaws are the Sese (beans), the Eligidi (pumpkin), the Esuro (antelope), the Ekun (rabbit), and the Eku ago or white-bellied rat which the Alafin of Oyo is seen at times to raise to his lips as if to kiss.

Two days after my visit to Akure, where I saw the people preparing to worship Eshu while at Ipetu, just after I had finished talking to the chiefs, dancers, singers and drummers, followed by a crowd, came prancing to my tent, in a cloud of dust, and I was informed that the followers of Shango were preparing to hold their feast. So in this district the feast of Shango follows close after, or about the same time as, that of Ifa. A very tall and graceful looking woman, a priestess of Shango, closely followed by a man, both rattling some seeds in a long-necked gourd, and three or four women attendants, commenced dancing in front of my tent. They said this woman represented Shango. She was dressed in a blouse of a dark colour and skirt of white. Over this skirt, hanging from her waist, she wore pieces of cloth and velvet six inches in width, and perhaps two feet in length. Her hair was dressed in a series of rolls running from her forehead to the back of

---

[1] Shango—Bishop Johnson says that he is a deity imported from the Niger. Col. Ellis says he is the son of Yemoja, the daughter of Odudua and Obatala. Oja called him the son of Oranyan. As pointed out by Idowa, Kuso near the town of Oyo is where Shango has his sacred grove. Mr. E. P. Cotton in his report on the Egba boundary says that Shango was the fourth king or Alafin of the Yoruba. According to the Ibadan hunter, Alara (the owner of thunder), was one of the 16 sons of Oranyan.

her head, the largest being near the crown of her head. I was told that she was collecting money towards the expenses of the coming feast. Generally seventeen days' notice are given, so that the feast of Shango in these parts, it will be noted, takes place at the beginning of the tornado season. During the festival the Odushushango dance, carrying pots of fire on their heads, and this fire they say cannot be quenched by water. The hair of these men is allowed to grow long and is arranged like a woman's. Although this of course gives them an effeminate appearance I am not able to attach any homosexual act to the custom. They certainly are credited with magical powers and they are rather honoured than hated.

SHANGO

Told by Mr. Pellegrin

Shango is a man like myself, and when young could not be controlled by his parents, so they left him to his rascality. He used to waylay people on the roads and kill them, so all the Orishas (201) tried to find him, each giving one man. They heard he was at Egbe. They met him there. He said he was tired of running away, he would see what they could do. Ogun said he would catch him, so he took his pincers and ran after him; then Shango sent Thunder against him, but Ogun caught her in his pincers. Shango said he could not allow anyone to catch him, so he left his bow at Egbe, and ran away. So he is called "Oja ja forun ti l'egbe," the man who fought greatly and left his bow at Egbe. Then all the 201 representatives went and told Odudua, their chief. Then Odudua ordered them to go back and catch him. They went, but he told them that they would not see him again, and he took a chain and knocked the earth, and it opened and he went below. He said they would hear of him for ever. Then they returned to tell Odudua, and he said as Shango had left the earth he was glad. Odudua took the Thunder from Ogun, and gave him a sword to kill anyone who came his way. Then they met to arrange who should go on earth to repair the damage Shango had done, and they elected Truth. And when he arrived he began to use his influence. When a child died he visited the parents and told them that as human beings they would all die. This kind of comfort they did not care for, so they sent to Odudua, and told him that Truth did not agree with them, so Odudua took Truth away from them. He asked them which Orisha they wanted, and they said the Iro (lie), who made images and carved eyes, nose, ears, mouth : they said he would have sense to rule over them. Odudua gave them Iro to rule them. And when one falls sick and goes to him he tells them to gather such and such a leaf, and make medicine and take it, and the fever will go away. If he hears anyone fighting he hears both sides, and settles it. When they saw that matters went well with them like this, the chief of them was called "Ajalorun" (See Ifa)—one who fights in heaven. This Ajalorun sent to Odudua and asked that the name of Iro should be changed to Orishala. Ajalorun and Odudua are of the same mother, Ajalorun being the younger. Ajalorun called Iro Orishala, alaba la she, iku pa ni pori. (Orishala means the great Orisha, Alabalashe, one who commands [the Balogun], Iku pa ni pori, Death kills us and kills the head). Then Orishala began to reign in the world, and made eyes, nose, mouth, ears, head, etc., for them all. And then the people began to hear Shango in heaven.

Shango

Told by Solako

Shango is Odudua's son and a rascal, and he ran away. Then Odudua sent to Oshala and Ogun, his sons, to find out the truth about Shango. And they fought with him, but they could not catch him; so they told Odudua. He used to cut a leaf and chew it, and then fire came out of his mouth, and people ran away. Then Odudua called a meeting, and asked who would catch him, and Ogun volunteered. He met him at Egbe. They fought: he left his bow there, and went to Kuso. Then they went to tell Odudua, and he said they must catch him, and so they went to Kuso, and Shango said he would not see them. He threw his chain to heaven, and it opened for him, and he disappeared. And there he thundered and lightened, and everyone began to worship him.

Oshun

Told by Shotundi of Abeokuta

Oshun is a woman slave of one Oshunmakide, whose name before being bought was Omujo. She then became Oshunmakide's second wife. The master first asked her what she could do, and she answered that the only thing she knew how to do was to dance, so he called her Omujo. And he allowed her to dance, and while doing so she displayed magical powers by changing her dress in the presence of everyone instantaneously. When the first wife saw this, thinking that her husband would love Omujo more than her, one day as she was dancing she used some charm and turned her into water. Then the husband and the people, thinking that this was part of her performance, waited, expecting her to resume her position as a woman. And when this did not occur the husband wept bitterly, and all the people went home. Afterwards the husband married another woman, and she bore him no children; then he went to the Babalawo and asked how this was. And he said, "You have got a woman that became water, and so the new wife must worship water before she can have a child; and they must call the water Oshun.[1] And when worshipping it she must call out 'Omujo logun rora gungoke, rora gun okuta :' O dancer warrior!

[1] Oshun is one of the principal rivers in Yorubaland.

go gently up the hill, go gently up the rock." And the wife worshipped Oshun in this way, and had children.

The Ewaw of the Yoruba.

J. G. Frazer, in an article, " Howitt and Fison," in "Folk Lore," Vol. XX., No. 2, page 179, referring to the Australian class system says : " But if the system was devised to prevent the marriage of brothers with sisters, of parents with children, and of a man's children with his sister's children, it seems to follow that such marriages were common before the system was instituted to check them ; in short, it implies that exogamy was a deliberate prohibition of a former unrestricted practice of incest, which allowed the nearest relations to have sexual intercourse with each other. This implication is confirmed, as Messrs. Howitt, Spenser and Gillen have shown for the tribes of central Australia, by customs which can be reasonably interpreted only as a system of group marriage or as survivals of a still wider practice of sexual communism. And as the custom of exogamy combined with the classificatory system of relationship is not confined to Australia, but is found among many races in many parts of the world, it becomes probable that a large part, if not the whole, of the human race have at one time, not necessarily the earliest, in their history permitted the practice of incest, that is, of the closest interbreeding, and that having perceived or imagined the practice to be injurious, they deliberately forbade and took effective measures to prevent it." According to information I have received, incest is still common in the Ibibio districts of Southern Nigeria, but any such practice has been more or less stamped out in the Yoruba country by the system of "Ewaw" evidently instituted by the priests of Ifa for that purpose, and now incest is connected in their minds, as a system, only on the occasion of the festivals of the farm Orishas already mentioned. It is true that on the death of the father the son is given one or more of his father's wives, but generally one who has not had children, the other wives being sometimes distributed among the other relations.

On the third day after the child is born the Ifa priest is called in to give the child its "Orisha and its ewaws." The Orisha is the child's object of worship, and it may not marry one of the opposite sex having the same Orisha, which thus becomes its chief "ewaw." This Orisha holds good as a family deity and ewaw for four generations, that is to say if the Orisha has been given anew to the child then it will be his son's, his grandson's, and his great-grandson's. His son then takes as his second ewaw his father's wife's animal ewaw. This one's son takes his father's wife's third or vegetable ewaw. And the latter's son takes his father's wife's fourth omen ewaw, *i.e.* a rat, bird, or snake.

The daughters take the father's Orisha, but, as the African says, if you wish to catch a rat you must go to its hole, or, in other words, in this case we must begin at the beginning.

The Yoruba divide people into six double or twelve single groups. The Fisherman, male and female. Fish, snakes, and birds, or omens, male and female. The Hunter, male and female. Animals, male and female. Farmers, male and female. Plants, male and female. In all six brothers and sisters, and all were of one family.

In the beginning brother married sister, or, in their words, eat[1] one another. For the sake of brevity we will number each of the six groups, and call each brother and sister by a letter. The Fisherman A, his sister B, the group 1. The Omens, male C and female D, the group 2. The Hunter, male E and female F, group 3. The Animals, male G, female H, group 4. The Farmer, male I, female J, group 5. Plants, male K, female L, group 6.

No. 1.	No. 2.	No. 3.	No. 4.	No. 5.	No. 6.
AB	CD	EF	GH	IJ	KL

But they soon got tired of this single diet, and the male product of AB caught the female product of CD ; EF of GH ; and so on.

| ABD | CDB | EFH | GHF | IJL | KLJ |

Even then they were not satisfied, and so the fisherman made war on the hunter, and the hunter on the farmer, and the farmer on the fisherman, and each appropriated the product of the other's labour. And the result was that the fisherman

---

[1] Je is to eat, dine ; owe ; deserve ; gain ; earn ; win.

eat flesh, the hunter eat vegetables and the farmer eat fish.

 ABDF CDBH EFHJ GHFL IJLB KLJD

Reprisals were made, and the fisherman took vegetables, the farmer flesh, and the hunter fish.

 ABDFJ CDBHL EFHJB GHFLD IJLBF KLJDH

This could not go on, so they called a great palaver, and finally agreed that they would give their daughters in marriage to one another, and now the priests see that there is no confusion nor disorder. While the wife shall be allowed to worship her Orisha it shall not be inherited by the son unless the Babalawo says it is time. By this the letters B D F H J L, as Orishas, drop out, but their blood remains as that of the group to which it belonged, and the ewaws stand

 ADFJ CBHL EHJB GFLD ILBF KJDH

Each person's ewaws shall in future be composed of one Orisha, one omen, one animal, and one plant. Each shall continue in the family for four generations, and shall then be renewed. Thus A C E G I K now drop out, and a male Orisha is needed to complete the ewaws. Number one or its product ADFJ can intermarry with Number two family, because their ewaws are all different: A and C may therefore enter each other's group: E and G may exchange: I and K also.

The families are now thus represented:

 DFJC BHLA HJBG FLDE LBFK JDHI

SHANGO—OYA—OBA—OSHUN

The next generation the letters D B H F L J.
Number one is now in want of fish, so he marries B of group No. 2.
Number 2 wants fish, and takes D.
Number 3 wants an animal, so he takes F.
Number 4 wants an animal and takes H.
Number 5 wants a plant, and takes J.
Number 6 wants a plant, so takes L.
The families now stand

    FJCB   HLAD   JBGF   LDEH   BFKJ   DHIL.

The letters F H J L B D now drop out.
Number one is now short of an animal, so he marries H.
Number 2 wants an animal, so takes H.
Number 3 needs a plant, so takes L.
Number 4 wants a plant, so takes J.
Number 5 desires fish, so takes D.
Number 6 needs fish, and takes B.
The groups now stand JCBH LADF BGFL DEHJ FKJD HILB.
And now J L B D F H drop out.
The male Orishas are now again to the fore: the groups stand

    CBHL   ADFJ   GFLD   EHJB   KJDH   ILBF

Now there are said to be 201 Orishas, and if for the sake of argument we say that 100 of these are male, you will see that there is ample scope for an enormous variation. There are also many omens, animals, and plants in use as marriage ewaws, as the list given below shows. I may say at once that their practice does not apparently agree with this theory. Presumably the groups mentioned acknowledged Olokun, Olosa, Ogun, Oshowsi, Oke, and Oko as their Orishas, and so group No. 1 is a male group, No. 2 a female, No. 3 a male, No. 4 a female, No. 5 a male, and No. 6 a female.

Such is, more or less, the idea that guides the Babalawos in their choice of Orishas and ewaws, but as we know there is always a vast difference between the ideal and the actual.

A native called Shoremekun, said to be an authority on this subject, informed me

(1) That the Orisha, given three days after birth when the father acknowledged the child as his before all the world, must be one that has been in the family.

(2) That no one could marry anyone of the opposite sex who might have the same Orisha.

(3) That all the daughters take the Orisha of the father.

(4) *a.* That he may not marry his uncle or aunt's "Ebi," on his father's or mother's side.

(*b*) He may not marry his brother's or sister's "Ebi."

(*c*) That by Ebi he meant

Omo Iya } his father's and mother's children.
Omo Baba }
Omomi   his own children.
Omomome   his grandchildren.
Omolala   his great-grandchildren.

Then he said that he had taken his mother's Orisha, which was Shango, and that his eldest son, grandson, and great grandson would all have Shango as their Orisha.

Next he went on to say that his father's name was Osho, and that his wife's name was Elekude, and that her Orisha was Orishako.

His grandfather's name was Nagulo, and his Orisha was Orishako[1]: he married Shabeyi, whose Orisha was Beji. His own wife's name was Moshalo, and her Orisha was Beji.

He had three brothers Shashino, whose Orisha was Ifa, Akikumi, whose Orisha was also Ifa, and Ojé, whose Orisha was Oro. And his sons were Adikunle, whose Orisha was Shango; Adinakon, a Christian who had no Orisha; Bamibopa, a Mohammedan, whose Orisha used to be Obatala, and Ladile, whose Orisha was Obatala.

His daughters' names were Shangoedi, Adinoju, Aditutu, and Shuboola, whose Orisha was Shango.

We note from the above that all brothers do not take the same Orisha. Shoremekun's father was not the eldest son of his grandfather, and therefore did not take the latter's Orisha. Neither was Shoremekun the son of his father's first wife Elekude. Shoremekun has given us the names of the chief wife of each of his ancestors only.

But this study is one that can be only taken up by someone who has unlimited time at his disposal, and I only give the above example to show how anyone,

[1] Orishako is in full Orisha Oko.

who forgets that a native may have any number of wives, may easily find sufficient apparent contradictions to cause endless confusion to any theory he may deduce from casual observation.

We have been told that theoretically each person should have one Orisha and three ewaws : well, from the following list you can form your own opinion as to the correctness of that theory or the present existing confusion. My sympathy is entirely with the patient priests of Ifa, whose duty it now is to enquire into the genealogies of all newly-born infants, and to assign to them what we now perhaps look upon as our armorial bearings.

In the following lists I give, under the name of his Orisha, first, the man's name, secondly, his town, thirdly, what he must sacrifice to his Orisha, fourthly his ewaws or things forbidden to him, and fifthly, whether he may marry one with his Orisha or not.

ORISHA OGUN.

Name.	Town.	Sacrifice.	Ewos or Ewaws.	Yes.	No.
Ogunkula	Ijaiyi	Dog, beans	Ground nuts, Efaw, awsawn, a vegetable, and the cricket		1
Alowani	Offa.	Dog, beans	May not eat the sacrificed dog, but only taste the water in which it has been boiled. Efaw, awsawn and banana		1

ORISHA OGUN.—*Continued.*

Name.	Town.	Sacrifice.	Ewos or Ewaws.	Yes.	No.
Osho	Abeokuta	Dog, bean bread, pounded yams, palm wine	Snake, the leaf of Ogunmo		1
Alabi	Akure	Dog, palm oil, salt	None	1	
Ajibola	Ibadan	Dog, kola, palm wine, roasted and pounded yams	Fowls, adultery		1
Ajala	Ibadan	Dog, goat, sheep	Fowls		1
Lanloyi	Ogbomosho	Dog	Personal Ewaw dog		1
Kale	Awyan	Dog, beans, all fried things	Ire (Funtunsia Elastica)		1
Ogundipe	Ogbomosho	Dog, corn, pigeon	Ire	1	
Aborishade	Ijero	Dog, palm wine	None	1	

EGUN.

Amodu	Abeokuta	Cock, ram, beans	Not to reveal secrets		1
Akiwanmi	,,	Goat, fowl	(Red monkey) Iji		1

BAYANI OR BAYONI.

Badamosi	Abeokuta	Cow, fowl, palm oil, yams	Dog, pig, roasted yams, pito, palm wine. May not carry water		1

IFA.

Name.	Town.	Sacrifice.	Ewos or Ewaws.	Yes.	No.
Fumiwirji	Akure	Pig, Goat, Fowl, bandicoot	Fish, dog. May not carry nor bail water		1
Komolapi	Ilesha.	Pig, goat, fowls, bandicoot, pounded yams	Dog, pig, tete (vegetable)	1	
Ojo	Offa	Goat, fowl, bandicoot, tortoise	Sheep, oyo leaves, banana	1	
Alade	Ibadan	She goat, pounded yams	Cock, goat, Okro, adultery on the wife's part	1	
Ojuola	Oyo	Pig, goat, fowl, pounded yam and beans (egusi)	Rats, dry fish, partridges, eggs, ducks, efon (veg.), palm kernels		1
Makidi	Abeokuta	Goat, fowl, pounded yams	Dog, pig		1
Ashaolu	Akure	Goat, bandicoot fish, snail	Igi, Isin (no fire)		1
Shotunde	Abeokuta	Goat, fowl	None	?	?

ORISHA OYA (AWYA).

Ige	Offa	Fowl, pounded yams, goat and Ishapa soup	Sheep and cow		1
Makunde	Ibadan	Fowl, goat, pounded yams, pito (beer)	Sheep, ram		1
Oyadeji	Abeokuta	Fowl, pounded yams	Sheep, snail, elephant, dog		1

ORISHA OYA (AWYA)—*Continued.*

Name.	Town.	Sacrifice.	Ewos or Ewaws.	Yes.	No.
Belo	Abeokuta	Fowl, goat	Sheep, efon antelope		1
Awyalola	Ibadan	Fowl, goat, yams	Sheep		1
Sumanu	Ikirun	Fowl, goat, kola	Sheep	1	
Adeoti	Offa	Fowl, goat	Sheep	1	
Awyawerni	Ikirun	Fowl, goat, pounded yams	Sheep, beans		1
Abiawna	Ibadan	Fowl, goat	Sheep		1

SHANGO.

Name.	Town.	Sacrifice.	Ewos or Ewaws.	Yes.	No.
Idawo	Ibadan	Ram, fowl	Antelope (Eshuo), rabbit (Ekun), pigeon pie		1
Lajidi	Ijaiyi	Ram, fowl	Antelope (Eshuo), rabbit (Ekun), rat (Ago), dog		1
Abidogun	Ibadan	Ram, kola, cold water	Rat, dog		1
Shangotola	Abeokuta	Dry fish, beans, yams	Sheep, hedgehog, armadillo, antelope, alligator, tortoise		1
Adeyauju	Ibadan	Ram	Rat, beans (sese), antelope		1
Bangbola	Ibadan	Ram, kola, cock, yam	Rat, beans (sese)		1
Shangotayo		Ram, fowls, kola	Rat, beans (sese)		1

ORISHALA, OBATALA, OSHALA, ORISHANLA, OSHANLA.

Name.	Town.	Sacrifice.	Ewos or Ewaws.	Yes.	No.
Olorishade	Abeokuta	Snail, kola, yams, fowl, goat, ducks, pigeons	Dog, palm wine, may not use brass	1	
Adeoye	Ibadan	Snail, fowls, ducks, pigeons, yams	Dog, palm wine, tortoise	1	
Laleye	Ogbomosho	Fowl, yam, egusi soup	Salt, palm wine, palm oil, may not sleep on mat	1	
Adelafun	Ilorin	Snail, egusi, yam	Salt, palm oil, palm wine, pepper	1	
Adeshiyan	Ibadan	Snail cooked with shea butter, fowl	Palm wine, corn wine and snuff	1	
Adedoja	Ikirun	Snail, fowl	Palm wine	1	
Aborishade [1]	Ijero	Snail, goat, kola, akara	Dog, palm wine	1	
Adeyola	Ibadan	Snail, fowl, Ori	Palm wine		1

ESHU.

Momodu	Otton Oshoybo	He goat	Nut oil, onions, dog	1	
Ojo	Ede	He goat, sheep	Nut oil, dog	1	
Adekunbi [1]	Iganna	He goat, dog, pig	Nut oil		1

ODUDUA.

| Lowale | Ife | Sheep, palm wine | None | 1 | |

Orisha Oko, Oshaoko.

Name.	Town.	Sacrifice.	Ewos or Ewaws.	Yes.	No.
Akitundi	Ijanji	Dried meat, egusi, yams	Antelope, and may not eat new yams before Oko's festival		1
Obasa	Ido	Snail, fish, ekuru beans	Butter kola	1	
Adekunbi [1]	Iganna	Goat, fowls, fish, rat	New yams	1	

Shankpana, Shankpano, Shakpana.

Name.	Town.	Sacrifice.	Ewos or Ewaws.	Yes.	No.
Aminu	Abeokuta	Sheep, beans, palm oil	Yamati seed, tobacco, not to sit on mortar, head not to be knocked.		1

Oshun.

Name.	Town.	Sacrifice.	Ewos or Ewaws.	Yes.	No.
Salami	Abeokuta	Rats, gala (antelope), corn, yams, palm oil	Etu (antelope), fowl, palm wine, beans		1
Oyiwopo	Offa	Goat, fowls	Pito (corn beer)		1
Babatunde	Abeokuta	Goat, fowls, beans, youri (veg.)	Pito, snail, elephant	1	
Akande	Ibadan	Rabbit, antelope, dry fish, yams, pito	Rats, he goat, cocks, snails, ducks, ground corn, water yams		1
Tinuola	Ilaro	Corn with oil	None	1	
Adederan	Ikirun	Goat, fowl	Corn wine	1	

Ibeji.

Name.	Town.	Sacrifice.	Ewos or Ewaws.	Yes.	No.
Kaiwo	Ibadan	Fowl, beans, yams and oil, kola.	Monkey		1
Kainde	Oyan	Ekuru beans, all fried things	Nut oil, Ire (Funturia elastica)		1

ERINLE.

Name.	Town.	Sacrifice.	Ewos or Ewaws.	Yes.	No.
Ishola	Ijaiyi	Cock, beans, butter, kola, yam flour, pounded yams, agidi	elephant and hippo		1
		ORI.			
Adeniji	Abeokuta	Fish, beans (egusi)	New yams before the Oko festival	1	
		YEMAJA or YEMOJA.			
Adeniran	Ibadan	Yams, palm oil, cooked corn, yam flour	Dog, alligator, unskinned roasted beef		1
Abiara[1]	Ibadan	Sheep, fowl, snails	Dog		1
		AGBA.			
Fabode[1]	Oyan	Dog, fowl, goat	Palm wine, dried okro	1	
		AGA.			
Fabode[1]	Oyan	Fowl goat	Ebolo and Odu herbs	1	
		OBALUAYE.			
Abiara[1]	Ibadan	Goat, fowl, snail	Beniseed		1
		OKEJEMORI.			
Oke	Ibadan	Snail, fowl	Dog, palm wine		1
		ORO.			
Asani	Abeokuta	Ram, corn wine	Dog, horse		1

[1] It will be noted that some people now have two Orishas.

Many in these lists may marry women who have their Orishas, but they could give me no reason for this. It is possible that certain people of royal descent may marry whom they like.

In Ibadan I have been told that in the olden times twins had to marry twins.

SHANGO—OYA—OBA—OSHUN

Orishas of Birth, Life and Death

We have left to us the Orishas Oba, Shankpana and Dada, whose other name is Bayoni or Bayani.

Oba or Ibu is the third wife of Shango, and represents the thunder of Shango, the meeting of the clouds and the crying out. The word Ibu also means the one who broils or bakes under ashes, and thus this Orisha may be said to be the wife that first made native bread. But I was told that Oshun was the woman bread-maker. I am inclined to think that there has been some confusion in the occupation of Shango's wives, who are said to stay at home, as the meaning of Shango's third wife's name so evidently points to Ibu or Oba as the bread-maker.

About Dada, the Orisha of Birth, things created and vegetables, we know very little. Ellis tells us that he is represented by a calabash ornamented with cowries, on which is placed a ball of Indigo.

As to Shankpana a story tells us that:—

> Erinle and Shankpana are offspring of Shango and Oya. Shankpana was a wicked boy, and Erinle was his sister. When they were young Erinle used to warn him not to be cruel to people's children, because he was accustomed to beat them. Shankpana asked her why she cared for other people's children. Erinle said she liked to have plenty of companions to play with. Shankpana said he did not like these crowds of children, so he went on beating them, and made the parents cry. Then she went and told her father, Shango, of how Shankpana treated children, and Shango sent for him and beat him. Shankpana

then said he would revenge himself on Erinle, and when he next saw her he flogged her to death, and took her to the bank of a river, and buried her there. After seventeen days, as the parents had not seen Erinle, they began to search for her, but could not find her; and Shankpana said nothing. Then they consulted the Babalawo, and he told them that Erinle had been killed and buried on the bank of the river, and, as she died for her love of children, anyone who wanted children must worship Erinle on the bank of the river. And so she became an Orisha to be worshipped on the bank of any river.

Erinle means elephant that flourishes on the land. Elephant is something that is great and loving.

And Shango drove Shankpana into the bush, and there he became a mysterious and harmful bushman, throwing smallpox and sickness about.

"The word Shankpana means one that cuts and kills one on the road. Oba was his real name—a title given to him as one who should look after, and be a leader among, children."

We have now connected all the children of Yemoja with all the occupations [1] of the primitive Yoruba, and as we were led to expect they fall into their places under the six or seven great categories.

(1) Dada   things made, created, birth, etc.
(2) Water   the fisherman and his Orishas, Olosa and Olokun.

---

[1] It must be remembered that Ifa is said to have chosen his disciples, or councillors, from all parts of the country. The fact of his having chosen Olokun and Olosa proves that the dwellers by the sea must have been included.

(3) Earth	the hunter and Oshowsi and Ogun.
(4) Fire and marriage	the priest farmer, and Oke and Shango.
(5) Motion and conception	the farmer and first harvest, and Oshun and Oko.
(6) Energy, Weight Pregnancy	women and all the people, and Oya and Ajeshaluga.
(7) Life and Death, Suffering	all folk, and Oba and Shankpana.

Thus these Orishas in their order and meaning agree with the Odus or sacred palm nuts in the order given to me by the priest Oliyitan. These categories also are thus identical with those I discovered to be at the back of the mind of the Bavili in the Congo. And the heavenly and earthly forms of Government, office for office, or rather official for Orisha, also coincide. And as the occupations of the Yoruba are followed according to the seasons of the year, it follows that the Orishas of the different professions should also appear to rule certain seasons.

In the earliest period of man's existence, the period from marriage to birth and the problems involved seem to have occcupied his attention, and as he was driven to shelter by the first rains, and that was the time of marriage, the rain season was of the greatest importance to him, hence his primitive calendar of eight rain months. As he progressed in civilisation so did his sense of time, until Ifa, or some great philosopher, fixed his primitive observations, and gave him his present lunar calendar. It seems to me that there can no longer, now, be any doubt about either the order or form of the ancient West African social and religious system.

In Chapter XII. I have connected the leopard with the Alafin, and given the insignia by which one may recognise the head of the Yoruba people. The sign of office of the Alake, the head chief of the Egba, is a crown of beads.

In the olden days in the Congo, that is before European control existed, we had to be very careful in regard to etiquette in our relations with the chiefs. As wearers of boots we white men ranked with the highest in the land, and could command the respect due to our station, if not our deserts. I remember on one occasion, shortly after my arrival on the coast, being called and treated by a rich native trader as a "small boy" (a person of no importance). Well, we had no armies or force of our own by which to maintain our authority, so we had to rely upon the goodwill of our native chief. On this occasion the chief was called down, and three chairs were placed in the yard in front of the house. The chief who, for the occasion, wore boots, sat in the centre chair, and I sat in the chair on his right. The wicked native who had dared to call me a "small boy" was invited to put on a pair of boots and sit in the vacant chair. He ran away, and so lost the "palaver," and was fined. And when we called the chiefs in to settle some question or other, we had to place so many chairs with pieces of cloth upon them for the greater chiefs to sit on, and to spread mats on the ground for the lesser chiefs, while, rich or poor, the rest of the courtiers or followers sat on the earth.

I find much the same custom exists in Abeokuta.

(1) The Alake, of course, and his three courtiers have the right to Agas, or chairs.

(2) The Iyalode has the right to an Aga, but her three courtiers sit on mats.

(3) The Balogun, whose sign of office is his armour, has the right to a chair. Two of his courtiers, Bada and Seriki, have the right to Agas, but Ashipa sits on a mat.

(4) The Bashorun, whose sign of office is a large umbrella and a staff of beads, has the right to a chair, but his officers sit on mats.

(5) The Ogboni are distinguished by their leather bags, a long walking-stick or staff, and the horse's tail which they carry on their shoulders.

Each chief in his own quarter used to settle disputes and woman palavers.

When there was a misunderstanding among the members of the Ogboni, all the members of the craft assembled and settled it.

The Ogboni tried all murder cases, and, as has been shown, had to do with funerals. The head of each occupation and his council, such as hunters, farmers, priests, market women and crafts, settled the palavers touching such occupations. But when death from sickness or famine raged in the town, the King, nobles, chiefs, and all the people held a general meeting. Divination took place, and evildoers were sought out and punished, or killed as a sacrifice to their outraged Orishas.

Such was what may be called the Home Government of the Yoruba, but as conquerors these people have progressed a little beyond this, for as victors the head chief appointed Ajele, or Governors, in the conquered provinces. These regents, while acting as tax-gatherers, interfere as little as possible with the home affairs of their districts. A glance at the following chapter on the land laws in the Western Province of S. Nigeria, or Yorubaland, will show the place more or less which these Ajele occupy.

CHAPTER XVII

LAND LAWS [1]

IN a paper which appeared in the *African Journal*, page 312, No. III, April, 1902, "a native of Yoruba gave an interesting account of the 'Native System of Government and Land Tenure in the Yoruba Country.'" In this paper he states:

"All lands in the country are in the keeping of chiefs for the members of the tribe to whom the land belongs. There is not a foot of land that is not claimed or possessed by some tribe or other, and the members of each tribe can apply to their respective chiefs for a grant of land to be used and cultivated for farming or other purposes. Any land so granted becomes the property of the grantee for life and for his heirs after him in perpetuity with all that grows on it *and all that lies under it.* (?) [2] But such land must be made use of; *i.e.* it must be cultivated or used beneficially, if not, the grantee is liable to lose it, and it may then be given to another who will make use of it.

---
[1] By kind permission of the African Society.
[2] (?) Mine R.E.D.

"No land is granted for pecuniary consideration; that is, no land is given for so much money. A man to whom land is granted may make a present to the grantor *if he so chooses*; that is merely a private gift.

"In this way every piece of land is owned by someone or other, and the boundaries are generally definite and clear.

"In the native system of Land Tenure not even a King has a right to alienate any land from him to whom it has been granted, unless indeed the man is guilty of negligence or lawlessness, as above stated: and even then it is the chief who has granted the land 'who dispossesses the grantee.

"It is important to note that the idea of selling land is entirely foreign to the native system."

In *Land Tenure in West Africa*, Reports by T. C. Rayner, Esq., Chief Justice of Lagos, and J. J. C. Healy, Esq., Land Commissioner, Chief Justice Rayner writes—" The question as to how the land, which in my opinion all originally belonged to the King or head chief of the country, became divided up among the various persons now owning it is not always easy to discover: and the difficulty is increased when we remember that according to strict native ideas land is absolutely inalienable. I believe that the notion that land can be sold, or given in such a way that the original owner loses all interests in it, is utterly foreign to the natives of all this coast.

"There is no time limit during which the grantee may occupy: he can occupy in perpetuity, but should he quit the land it reverts to the owner, and in certain cases the owner can eject him, *e.g.* if he claims the land as his and denies the grantor's right, or if he attempts to sell the land. The grantor regards the land still as his, subject to the grantee's right to occupy, and so long as *he pays his rent* [1] (or tribute, as it is more usually called) the grantee can go on occupying, and his heirs after him without interference. The rent or tribute is required and paid in the case of a stranger, simply as an acknowledgment of the grantee's title; it bears no relation to the value of the land, and is in all cases quite nominal. I think there can be no doubt that originally, according to native law, land was inalienable,[2] and that the chief or head of the community was the only person who could be said to be the owner of the land."

The statements of an individual must always be looked upon as more or less an expression of the impression he has obtained from the more or less restricted field of his labours.

[1] See further on, where natives who have bought land declare that they have not to pay tribute.

[2] *Note.*—(MSS. Mr. E. P. Cotton, L.S., B.E., F.R.A.S., Director of Surveys, S. Nigeria.)

The inalienability of land is firmly rooted in the Yoruba mind. If he is convinced that his ancestors at one time owned a certain piece of land, the remoteness of that ownership, or the validity of the present owner's title, appears to be no bar to his title.

The chiefs of country towns and villages do not understand the principles of modern land alienation. These chiefs are quite prepared to allot land to members of the community, or even to strangers, *so long as* they receive in return some *small periodical payment, generally in kind*, as an acknowledgment of title. The grantee may occupy the land for any length of time, but should he attempt to sublet, or dispose of it in any other way the grantor may at once eject him.

It is under the latter category that I would submit the following notes.

It would appear that before native Governments were organised and village life was more in evidence, every individual enjoyed the right of taking unoccupied land as much as he could use, wherever and whenever he pleased. This was afterwards deemed his property as long as he cared to keep it in use, and after that it again became common property, and, according to D. R. Campbell in *A Pilgrimage to my Motherland*, this custom was observed by all the Aku (Yoruba),[1] and I know that in some districts in the Central Province hunters settled on so-called waste land and had families, and the members of these families planted where they liked, as Mr. Campbell says all the Aku did in 1861.

The land question may be said to commence when the rights of fishing in reaches of rivers were first looked upon as belonging to certain fishermen, and when hunters commenced to assert their rights to certain lands as theirs for hunting purposes.

First Development.—But as the villages grew, and farming operations extended, farms of one fisherman's or hunter's family met the farms of another fisherman's or hunter's. Then disputes and little wars took place until some agreement between the two families fixed their respective boundaries. In this way came about the regulation of farming operations by the head of

[1] Aku is probably a corruption of the word Eko, the name of the people of Lagos. Eko would probably be the name given in Sierra Leone to people coming from Lagos, and so to Yoruba generally. Hence perhaps the Kroo boys' word for the Yoruba Nagu.

the family or Bale. We have instances of this in small villages in the Benin city territories.

Second Development.—Disputes occurred about standing plants such as bananas, and at last it became a custom for a farmer to claim the land as long as anything on it that he had planted bore fruit.

Third Development.—In time, powerful families conquered their weaker neighbours, and at last we have the land spoken of as belonging to some great chief. These chiefs extended their kingdoms, until we have powerful native states such as that of Benin governing many families of different origin. This kingdom was governed by the Oba and Council through Ogies[1] in the Benin kingdom. And these Ogies, residing generally at the capital of the conquered families as representatives of the conquering Oba, had the power to distribute land among the many families under them, all land now being looked upon, at least theoretically, as belonging to the Oba. And thus what may at one time have been looked upon as waste land in a province or kingdom became the property of the Oba. In the case of the kingdom of Benin, these waste lands were from time to time distributed amongst the King's sons, who thus became Ogies, *paying yearly tribute to the Oba.*

In Yorubaland theoretically all the land belongs to the Alafin of Oyo, and the chiefs of the so-called independent peoples certainly at one time paid tribute to him.

---

[1] Kongo zovo in the Congo, Ajele in Yorubaland.

Fourth Development.—After many years of provincial warfare and European intervention, we find Yorubaland divided into two great divisions, (1) The Protectorate and (2) the Colony of S. Nigeria (lately Lagos).

The Protectorate in the Western Province may be said to be formed of the Oyo, Elesha, Ife, Ibadan, Egba, Ijebu, and Ondo protected native states.

The Supreme Court has power and jurisdiction in each of these states for the administration and control of the property and persons of all persons *not being natives of each individual state*, that is, of aliens in the restricted sense of the word, but it has no control apparently over the property of the natives in each state, so that here, at any rate, land disputes are heard and judged by the natives themselves according to native law, or its abuse, as the case may be.

Fifth Development.—1. In that part of Yorubaland where the Alafin holds direct sway, old customs are conserved far more strictly that in the other states where the people have more power, and the sale of land, although not unknown, is rare It occurs at times when the claim to succeed to the ownership of land is disputed. As a way out of the difficulty, the farm is sold and the yield divided between the claimants. But the Alafin has the right to step in and take away the land from the family and give it to whom he likes. This is seldom done, but it is possible.

The custom of buying and selling land is gradually becoming more common, but it is much rarer here than in other states where more kola and palm trees are planted.

2. In Ibadan the custom of selling land, it appears, has crept in through the depravity of certain owners of farms and the necessity of their paying back money that has been borrowed.

(a) Moredaiyo of Ibadan, in answer to my questions, gave me the following information :—

The Alafin is looked upon as owner of all the land. The Bale of Ibadan received some land from the Alafin, but he has added to it greatly by conquest. The Bale took the land from the conquered people, and it now belongs to him. After making many of the conquered people slaves, some of those who had escaped returned to their towns under an Ajele appointed by the Bale, such as the towns of Ijaiye, Awaiyi, Iwahun, Okeamu, Ilesan, Takiti, Gbagba, Gangan, Tide, Ijebure, Otun Iyapa, Iro, Isi, Ileje, Omujelu, Oyife, Okeako, Tapati, Egbe, Nikinyinrin, Okeapa, Olofashan, Oye, Aiyidi, Imesin, Ikogusi, Ifewara, Itaogbolu, Ilofa ; but other towns that had chiefs with titles recognised by the Alafin, such as Ife, Elesha, were left alone.

If anyone in the towns with an Ajele [1] wanted land, he would go to the Ajele with a present (20 heads of cowries = 10/-) and ask for what he wanted. If the Ajele agreed, he would take him to the land and mark the boundaries in proportion to the number of retainers the petitioner brought with him.

---

[1] This implies that the conquered land belongs to the conqueror and does not remain in the hands of the conquered chief.

When the Ajele gives the land he makes the petitioner promise not to fight or disobey the law, or the land will be taken from him.

The petitioner now becomes an Onile (or one who has land).

The boundaries are cut, and heaps of earth are made at intervals, and on these a peregun tree is planted.

Every year, as a thank-offering, the Onile gives the Ajele a present of that product which thrives best on the land.

The Onile now divides his land among his family and retainers and they become farmers, or Oloko (owners of farms). The Onile has the right to call on the Oloko to work for him for one or two days in the year, to fire the bush and prepare a place for him to farm, and the Oloko give the Onile a yearly present. The Onile may not sell the land to his retainers, he gives it to them and they legally have no right to sell it. It happens, however, that on the death of a father the son who has succeeded to the farm becomes a worthless spendthrift, and has had to borrow money from some rich man. This money-lender presses him for repayment, and the wicked son has told him to take the farm and cease bothering him. The Onile may if he likes interfere and drive such a wicked person out of his farm, and, if he has no son, or near relation, take the farm away and give it to someone else who, however, must pay the money-lender the sum borrowed. The money-lender cannot take possession without the consent of the Onile.

(b) Moredaiyo's father was an Onile, and gave a farm to one of his friends called Lesinpo. Lesinpo died. His son occupied the farm. He was a wicked person, and borrowed money and could not pay. For some years the money-lender lost sight of the farmer, and so he attempted to jump the farm. He did this by placing palm leaves on it. The Onile saw the palm leaves, and threw them away. The money-lender asked who had dared to displace the leaves. The Onile said he had, as the land was his. The money-lender then said "the farmer owes me money and he has gone away." He was told he had no right to take the farm for the money owed, as the farmer had relatives. The relatives paid the money-lender, and he recognised this and gave up his claim to the farm.

(c) Many Onile, if they have more land than they require, sell it to third parties, and the price varies from two bags, or 10s., to twenty bags of cowries, or £5. This buyer pays no yearly tribute, to the Onile or the Ajele, and the transaction is really contrary to the old customary law.

When one Bale succeeds another, he changes the Ajele and many of the customs of his predecessor.

So in the Ibadan territory, in spite of the fact that according to ancient law, land is inalienable, it has been pawned and sold for a long time, and is still being sold.

3. The selling of land with the consent of the chief in Ijebuland has reached such a pitch that

when I was last there, the chiefs were trying to prevent people from selling or buying land in a certain quarter of the town of Ijebu, which they held more or less sacred.

4. Mr. Pellegrin, an intelligent and educated Egba, gave me the following notes:—

"All Yorubaland belonged to the Alafin, but the Egba after the civil wars settled at Abeokuta, and by right of conquest took and kept possession of most of the land now known as Egbaland. In the conquered towns they generally placed an Ajele,[1] but left the chief in many cases in possession, exacting, however, a yearly tribute. Thus Otta, Agege, Isheri Igawn, and Iro belonged to the people known as Awuri, but now form part of Egbaland.

"Supposing natives in any of these districts wanted land, they would go to the Bale and ask him for it, and he, on receipt of twelve kola and one case of gin, would grant it on condition that they would abide by the laws of the country.

"One of the customs of the country was to give the Bale a small portion of the products of the land, and another was that he could not sell the land. When one of these farmers dies and his son does not care to occupy the land, the Bale can give the farm to another, otherwise, the farm

[1] NOTE.—Ajele have been known to grant land to Onile who have planted it up with cocoa and kola, and when the trees are bearing, endeavour to turn the Onile out, without fair compensation. A case of this kind not long ago came before the notice of the Resident of Ibadan, who insisted on a fair price being paid to the Onile by the Ajele. In this case the ancient land law, in view of modern agricultural development, became evidently unfair.

descends to the son. The occupier of this land can, in his turn, give a portion of the granted land to a friend or anyone other than an alien. He receives a present and something yearly from this person. But if this part that is given to a third party happens to be thick forest land, and the receiver has to clear it, the land becomes his, and as an Onile he can leave it to his son. This man may not sell the land, but he can give it to another person and receive the case of gin and twelve kola.

"A woman may own land. (See below daughter.)

"A slave may not own land, but he may have a farm on his master's land. In the event of the death of his master, the slave may become the property of any of the deceased's relations and be taken away, or he may be allowed to remain on the land and go with it to his master's successor. A slave who has farmed and redeemed himself becomes the owner of his farm.

"When the land is allotted, Akoko, Atori or Peregun trees are planted on heaps of earth, and serve as boundaries.

"The land does not belong to the family, but to the father, and, later on the son or daughter.

"By family is understood uncles, aunts, nephews, nieces on both the Obakan (father's) side, and the Iyekan (mother's) side. On the death of the father, the chief divides money, goods, slaves or other movable property among the family. This division is made in accordance with the amount spent by the individuals of the family during the death and funeral ceremonies, and also in accordance with the services rendered to the deceased during his lifetime.

"In the event of the owner leaving the farm without a representative for a long time he may at any time come back and claim it. But should he die while absent, and not have left any planted trees, and the chiefs have given the land to another, the son or his heir cannot lay claim to the land, which has merely been farmed (see Baba Numi's report later on). But in the event of there being any living trees planted by him on the farm, the son or heir may claim it. But these questions are decided on their merits."

Baba Numi, an old Egba, illiterate, but said to know all about Egba land laws, gave me the following account:—

"When a man asks for land, the first question to be considered is—'Is he a native or an alien?'

"If he is not an Egba, and goes to a man and asks for land, that man must take him to the chief of the district, Bale, Balogun or Osi. If they agree to give the stranger land, the Balogun is asked to take him and show him the land allotted to him. When he dies and has children, they can succeed to it. If the successor owes money, he can pawn the land with the Bale's consent, and the moneylender can take the farm if none of his relations redeem it, but neither he nor the moneylender can sell the farm.

"Supposing he is not a stranger, he must be the son of a father who has land. If the land is too small for the son in possession to divide, the Bale will grant him a portion of land which becomes his property. It is granted to him and his successors in perpetuity for his and their use, but he is not allowed to sell it. If he is in debt, the family censure him and pay his debts, but if his debt is too large for them to pay, they give their consent to his pawning the farm, and the moneylender, with the consent of the Bale, can take the farm.

"Pawning land is a very old custom in this country.

"The moneylender does not plant trees, or then plants them at his risk, as the family may redeem their farm at any time, and all the trees planted become the property of the original owning family.

"The selling of land has been done privately for a very long time; people do this without the chief's knowledge, and people look upon the new occupier as one who has been allowed to farm and live on the seller's land by his consent.

"Should it become known that an owner has sold his land, the seller gets into trouble, and is driven out of the country, *but the buyer is not punished, and is allowed to go on farming in peace.* If a man simply farms his land and plants no trees, and is not married, and goes away, and dies, his farm is given away to another, and should he have a son while abroad, and that son comes and claims the farm, he has no right to do so, and the farm continues in the possession of the occupier.

"If, on the other hand, the farmer had a son when he went away, and took him with him, and he died abroad, and his son came back and found his father's farm occupied, the Bale would call him and the occupier before him and ask the latter to give the former a portion of the land. The son, however, would have to allow the occupier to reap the fruit of any trees he had planted there, so it generally ended in the Bale giving the son another piece of land."

Such is some of the evidence which I have collated, and from this we see that, legally speaking, according to native customary law, land is inalienable, and that the sale of land is a crime against the state. But, on the other hand, land is sold and the buyer is left in possession.

CHAPTER XVIII

CONCLUSION

By the fear of death and the desire to propagate and live, the Yoruba's thoughts were driven to the study in nature of the phenomena that caused death, or helped him to live and propagate. And as they progressed, men in all lines of life, *i.e.* the fisherman, the hunter, the priest, the farmer, and, later on, the market women and the craftsmen, all aided in this search for the causes of life and death, and the true nature of the spirit presiding over them all. In this way it does not seem strange to me that, if man has developed from a non-speaking animal stage of existence to his present speaking and cultivated stage, his knowledge of things and his way of expressing his ideas should have also developed step by step. I am not wonder-struck that man, governed more or less by his senses and environment, should have instinctively built up trains of thought and ways of expressing them that have led native philosophers to divide their mythology into certain well-defined categories. But I admit that a philologist unaided by a long and great knowledge of the people whose language he may be studying, will find great difficulty in recognising these categories in any but a primitive language. I think that his studies may best be rewarded in Africa by a thorough investigation of some Bantu tongue, but even here the student will need a more or less "primitive mind" attitude to carry out his work.

Yemaja's, or Yemoja's, first offspring by her son Orungun was the sea Orisha, Olokun. In this word we have the idea of "murmuring." The first man, says another legend, was Obalofun, the first speaker. Among the Bavili, Zimini, a plural word, literally meaning the male and female Egos, comes to mean the swallower, and Zimini was the man of the sea. It seems, therefore, that we shall not be doing the West African a wrong by concluding that he looked upon his first parent as a creature from the sea.

(1) As a "merman," shall we say, he was ruled rather by instinct than by reason, and I may presume that he knew more about propagation [1] than about

[1] The doyen of the senses is that of smell in order of creation. Bishop Crowther gives the word Imu (Crowther) or Imaw for our word nose. This word also means "sense" in a general way, thus the sense of taste is written imu tawwo (towo). Without any accent over the last syllable imu means the act of drinking. With a grave accent ìmu means knowledge, science, mythology, philosophy. In connection with the word Hu (to germinate) it means Imuhu, to create. Combined with the words Bi (to beget) and Si (to be) in the word imubisi, it means propagation.

The offspring Awmaw (omo) that shines or is good (dan) means a virgin, omidan, another name for whom is wundia (probably a Hausa word), the one who gives pleasure. Thus virginity and purity gave pleasure to the ancient Yoruba. On the other hand, that which was lewd and bad he called Buburu, *i.e.* that which swelled and sent out an offensive smell. I need hardly remind my readers of the action of animals in this regard, and that we still talk of the fires of love and desire. The native has another word for to smell, "Gbōrun" (Crowther), which is connected with the idea of heat (Orun) and to rub (gbo).

association, and that for a long time this instinct occupied most of primitive man's attention. He lived on herbs and leaves.

At length we arrive at the stage when man busied himself with certain occupations.

(2) As a fisherman, or still very primitive man, the elements that he constantly braved and the natural phenomena that he noticed caused him to ponder and weigh things. The oft-recurring light and darkness, day and night, heaven and earth, sun and moon, heat and cold, the power of the murmuring waves of the sea, the fierce rushing of flooded rivers, their constant beating against the rocks, thunder, lightning, wild winds and torrential rains, marriage and birth, life and death; all these kept his receptivity at work.

We will now consider the sense of touch. The verb Kan is to touch, and Shaw is an adverb qualifying verbs of touching or dipping, and means "just a touch." The word Shawkan (Crowther) is to copulate. In this connection it is bad for us when our body aches, and an ache is "kan." On the other hand, when we are free from ache "Dida ara" it is good Dida ara = healthiness.

To behold is wo, and iwo not only means sight but also light and countenance. Primitive man, attracted by her beauty or countenance (iwo) pursued (de) woman and seduced (dewo) her. That which is (ewa) is beauty, while that which does not abide (ailewa) is ugliness.

The word to eat (je) means also to win. The idea of following (taw) beauty (iwo) apparently continues in the idea of taste (taw wo). That which is sweet, delicious, is called dun, while that which is nasty is compared to the tasteless husks of Indian corn (eri).

I have now given you the Yoruba idea of good and bad under the senses of smell, touch, sight, and taste, it is left to trace their idea of good and bad in a general sense. Well, the Yoruba, like the Bavili, looks upon that which produces as good, *i.e.* Da to create, Ara body, or Dara good. Its opposite Aidara means bad.

It is evident therefore that the Yoruba ideas of good and bad are associated with the moral emotions of that most primitive of all religions, which may be summed up in the words "Increase and multiply."

His knowledge of all these "powers" may have been, nay, certainly was, as primitive as he, but in his earliest stage of existence he commenced to associate these powers with the life he propagated as the chief causes of death. He soon learnt that he was all too impotent to fight these terrific powers, and so kept his ears open to catch the slightest sound that might betray their coming. Although these powers were the cause of death, the waters yielded to the fisherman fish as the food upon which he lived, and so the sea, the lagoon and the rivers, and the powers behind them, and the fish became in a way sacred to him. More lives would be lost in his search for food in the waters than anywhere else. Thus, at the foundation of religion, which commenced in the very earliest existence of propagating man and his fear of death, we have a sense of primitive gratitude to the waters that supplied him in this stage with food. And in this way these water spirits, Olokun and Olosa, became associated with that which quickened his sense of hearing. Sound (figured here by the mighty, murmuring Olokun, the giver of fish, salt, sweetness, wisdom, and by the rushing of the waters of the rivers, as they flow from the interior into the sea) is the great parent of this family or category of thought. His opposite is the Lagoon, the listener, the absorber, through whom the salt is made. As a "merman" he may have heard, made a noise, smelt, felt, seen and tasted, but he probably knew little or nothing of associating, in the same way as thinking man does, outside phenomena with his senses. This, I think, is the first principle that native philosophy points to, *i.e.* that animals were credited, figuratively speaking, only with the senses of smell, touch, sight and taste, and that the great difference between him and man is the way in which the latter developed his sense of hearing, and his powers of speech. Hence in the philosophy of the Bavili the ear is said to have been, in his making, the first thing formed in the womb.

(3) The next stage in the development of moral man is figured to us by the hunter, and the trees and herbs growing out of the earth. From trapping fish to trapping "meat" is quite a natural step. The lessons about the "powers" which the primitive fisherman learnt have been handed down, but whereas the fisherman looked to the "waters" for his food, on land the hunter has turned to the forests. Long before the hunter had bows and arrows, he probably killed animals[1] by piercing them with pointed sticks, or by beating them to death, or by throwing stones at them. The hunter must have developed a great many virtues, courage among the rest. And hunting and its risks must have been the chief cause of death. As he beat down animals, so he was beaten down by the Orisha called "Ogun" (the one who beats or pierces with a pointed stick). He learnt to mimic the cries of certain birds and animals to lure them to their death. Someone then lured him on to death. This was Oshowsi, or Oshu, the one who speaks, o, him, si, to (used always with a verb of

[1] In fact this manner of hunting and killing with pointed sticks, I am told by Mr. E. Torday, is still common in the interior of the Congo.

motion towards), the wife of Ogun. When a man or woman was killed by Ogun, some fault or want of virtue was given as the reason. Ogun in this way was soon looked upon as a great judge and executioner. Hunters became great fighters, and, after the discovery of iron, were armed with arrows, tipped with this metal beaten into shape by some follower of Ogun, known later on as the blacksmith. Wandering through the woods as the hunter did, he is said to have been captured by Aja and taught the use of herbs, and so became a medicine man. In a later "cycle" of development he tamed the young of animals he captured, which later bred and became domesticated. Ogun is not only the god of hunters, and implements of war, etc., but the word is also the name of the stone which acts as the blacksmith's anvil. Ellis tells us that the ground is sacred to him, because iron ore is found in it; he certainly is a kind of earth god, and we have noted that he takes Odudua's place as a day of the week, but I think it is rather through his connection with the hunter, whose sphere of action was on earth, as opposed to the fisherman's on water, that he and Odudua are known as earth Orishas. At any rate, under the category of earth we have ideas of virtue, reason, justice, speech, and medicine. The fisherman *associated* ideas of good and evil with his powerful Orishas, the hunter brought his brain to work in the problem, and reached the stage of *ideation*.

(4 and 5) The next great stages are so nearly connected with procreation and farming as to be almost

inseparable. Though they occupy the same seasons, we must remember that these two great occupations of the thoughts of primitive man belong, as stages, to two different cycles, in the first of which agriculture played no part, but as cycle follows cycle, and the same season and occupation reappear, man is forced to entertain thoughts of both at the same time.

The following diagram may make this more plain:—

		First Stage.		*Second Cycle.*	
Dry season	⎧⎨⎩		2 ⎫ 3 ⎬ Fisherman 4 ⎫ 5 ⎬ Hunter	Association Ideation	
Rain season, ancient calendar	⎧ ⎪ ⎨ ⎪ ⎩	1 ⎫ Mar- 2 ⎬ riage 3 ⎫ Concep- 4 ⎬ tion 5 ⎫ Preg- 6 ⎬ nancy 7 ⎫ Life ⎬ and 8 ⎭ Death 9 or 1 Birth	6 ⎫ 7 ⎬ Planting 8 ⎫ 9 ⎬ Germination 10 ⎫ 11 ⎬ Harvest 12 ⎫ ⎬ Putrefaction 13 ⎭ Storing	Imagination Impression Reproduction Construction	

The farmer now began to cultivate the many herbs which, year after year, he had found by experiment were good for food. Driven by the storms to shelter at the beginning of the rains he naturally wished to have his vegetable food growing near to his hut. Perhaps he first placed his shelter near to where the green stuff grew. He would notice that at the time the rains came these nature-sown crops began to grow. And it was at this time that he mated. The great heat just before the rains caused fire [1] to come, as he thought, from the hills, and this phenomenon he called Oke. Then came the storms and lightning, warning him that it was time to mate and seek shelter. In this capacity of watcher of the signs of the times of propagation he was acting as a primitive priest. As a farmer he, as head of the house (Bale), provided his ancestors and family with food. They needed fish, birds, reptiles, animals and vegetables.

In these 4th and 5th developments of thought, or categories, we have on the one hand ideas of heat, fire, smell of burning, imagination, love, marriage, planting and sowing; and on the other, which closely follows it, the first fruits of the contact of the waters of heaven and the heated earth, the cold brought by the cooling rains, the quenching of the fires, impression, satisfaction of desire, conception, germination, motion and the first harvest of the self-sown and now planted grain. In other words all the ideas contained in the Orishas, Oke and Shango, Oshun and Oko, occupied the minds of the married couple and the primitive priest farmer.

(6) And now we arrive at a period of plenty, when all trees are bearing fruit, figured by the market women and market places where the abundance of the products brought forth by the waters

---

[1] Before fire was used for cooking purposes and man knew how to make it, bush fires that are now lighted by men, would not occur until nearly the end of the dry season, when natural combustion took place.

and rains, fish, reptiles, birds, animals and vegetables were sold. And Ajeshaluga, as we have noted, is not only the Orisha of wealth, but also that of colour, which needs eyes and sight to recognise, and which is best represented by the snakes or rainbows Oshumare and Ere. I am told that the recognition of the different colours of the rainbow is a sign of a high stage of civilisation; well, this is the sixth development or category of thoughts, so that my informant is apparently confirmed in his statement. But "colour" means more to the Yoruba than hue and tincture, for to the word Awo (Awaw) they attach the meaning of outward appearance, fashion, likeness, similitude and image. The Yoruba call purple, Awo Aluko; indigo, Awo Elu (after the indigo plant); light blue, Awo Ojuorun, sky colour; green, Awo Obedo, vegetable matter on stagnant pools; yellow, Awo Pupa; red, Awo Pupayo, and another name for reddish purple Awo Pupa Rusurusu, or somewhat red colour. I am inclined to think that this interesting word Pupa, red, is derived from the word Po or Paw to be plentiful (fruit is most plentiful when it is ripe and red), hence the word Pon or Pawn to be red or ripe, or to get yellow.

Thus in this category we have ideas of reproduction, colour,[1] sight, pregnancy, weight, harvest, wealth, buying and selling.

[1] The idea of colour is first perhaps obtained from the Rainbow Oshumare, who is reported to be a great snake (tchama in the Congo). She is said to send her slave the python (Ere) to destroy towns and collect slaves and food for her, and is also said to come up above the edge of the earth to drink the pure water of the sky. In the Congo the six colours

(7) In this development we have a picture of death and suffering, destruction and construction, figured by

which they recognise are said to be six snakes (page 139 "At the Back of the Black Man's Mind"). These colours are also recognised by the Yoruba, who attach some significance to them. When a man in the Congo is grieving over some misfortune he is said to be swelling. We should express the idea by saying that he was weighed down by sorrow and crying. In Yoruba we find the verb Wú is to swell and to be sullen, while Wu without the accent is to howl like a dog. When the father dies his relations cry out Or'o Baba O, so that all the people near may know that the head of the family is dead, and then the mourners do not wash, and dress in dirty dull red cloth, their nearest approach to purple, and so show their respect and fear of the departed. And people seeing this sympathise with them. The Yoruba call purple Awo Aluko, or the colour of a bird called Aluko. As we have noted, burials are very costly affairs in Yorubaland, and much money is needed.

Money or wealth is also needed for the purpose of purchasing things in the market, to pay the priests they call in to divine for them, to make presents to their chiefs, and to offer sacrifices to their Orishas of harvest, to propitiate the Orisha of sickness, and to thank their Orishas of birth.

It is a remarkable fact that the prevailing colour in the markets, as that of the wearing apparel of the market women, is indigo blue, and its popularity is due to the fact that the wearing of cloth of this colour indicates that the wearer is fairly well-to-do.

Now weighty matters are discussed in these markets, and the sharp wits of buyers are pitted against the cunning of the seller, but tne most noticeable feature is the noise caused by the people talking to one another. And so the ideas of intelligence, speech and understanding are connected with the market and the Indigo colour.

Another weighty matter, as all will recognise, is Religion. Now the priests of Ifa, I am told by Mr. Taylor, wear light blue cloths,[1] and I have also noticed more than one instance of a Babalawo dressed in cloth of this colour. These priests who play so great a part in marriage believe that they are inspired, and their grave demeanour impresses this fact upon the people. Theirs, in the olden days, was the office of smelling out witches, and they are still held in great respect as Diviners. And so this heavenly colour is connected with Inspiration, and the sense of smell, Divination and Religion or Marriage.

Green silk is the favourite colour of great chiefs, and the colour is symbolical of the season of conception and budding, or Spring. The ordinary individual may not touch the sacred person of a great chief or

---

[1] See also chapter VIII, page 96.

Shankpana or Buruku, sometimes written Buluku, and Oba or Ibu. Shankpana is in the first place the slayer of children, in the second the smallpox Orisha. Bulu is to blow vehemently upon, as the tornados blow upon the trees, etc., but the verb Bu is not only to spoil through damp, to decay, but also to broil or bake under hot ashes; Ru to rise, swell, boil over, and Kaw or Ku to construct; Ibu, the name of the river sacred to Oba, means she that bakes, or decays. In connection with these meanings we have to remember that these Orishas in the cycle represent the seventh and eighth months, the two tornado months finishing the rain season. In propagation these months are much feared, as children born now are more often than not still-born. Then fallen fruits damped by the rain and heated by the sun swell up and rot. I cannot, of course, say definitely that from this nature-process primitive man first learnt how to make his bread or pounded mass by heating and beating (Bulu is also to beat), but one of the wives of Shango is said to have been the first bread-maker, and they now boil cereals or yams, and then pound them

Oba, and so the ideas of Authority, the sense of touch and conception, are connected with the green of springtime.

The farmers watch the green corn turn yellow and ripe for harvest, and show their wisdom and discernment in its ingathering and disposal, and so wisdom, discernment, the sense of sight, and the yellow colour of the time of harvest are connected.

Then comes the time when all fruits are ripe, and the predominating colour is orange. This, especially in the olden days, was a time of great feasting, tasting and appreciation, and discrimination, for all fruits were not good, many of them being harmful if not poisonous.

And, finally, the last harvest was connected with the time of birth, and the gathering of the red coloured palm nut, and in the disposal and harvesting of this crop the farmers and traders had to use their powers of calculation, sense and judgment.

in a mortar to make what serves them as bread, and the meanings of the words Buluku and Ibu point in that direction. In this season also the angry winds blow down old trees and many branches, all of which would burn easily and are still preferred as firewood. This period then seems to have been one of destruction and construction, and as it developed gave birth to makers of bread, potters, hut and canoe builders, blacksmiths, weavers of cloth. The verb Towo (Tawwo) not only means to taste, but also to anticipate; and the word is composed of Taw to correct, educate, and Wo which means to fall down as a tree or fruit, or Wó to see, which seems to me, if we take into consideration the above meanings of the Orishas and the season of the year, that the Yoruba's idea of taste commenced when he first tickled his palate with the juicy fruits of trees that had fallen to the ground. This is perhaps made clearer when we find that (1) The words for palate are Imo (Imaw) Itowo (Itawwo) the sense of taste; (2) that the verb Mo means to drink, and (3) that Imo comes to mean notion, knowledge, wisdom, science, philosophy, etc.

It seems to me that man having no more senses could not progress further in this direction which, for the sake of clearness, I will call the perpendicular direction of the cycle, but in a parallel way development appears to be indefinite as season follows season.

(1) Thus from primitive man's sense of hearing correctly he progresses through many stages of civilisation to that of the right hearing which

we all connect with our Court of Equity and Arbitration.

(2) From a primitive power of forming ideas he marches on to right thinking, reason and justice, and Courts of Justice.

(3) From his sense of smell and imagination his primitive superstition may take him through different phases of marriage and of love to an at-one-ment with a true spiritual God, which we ourselves have not yet reached.

(4) His sense of touch and impression may carry him, step by step, from the fear of touching his sacred kings and rulers to obedience to law and order, and a desire to serve his king and country, and ideas of State.

(5) Through sight, colour and weight, the people may proceed little by little from their primitive and impulsive meetings in the market places, and a representative Council or Ogboni, to more and more civilised meetings and discussions of the affairs of the people in a great and more perfect House of Commons than any that yet exists.

(6) And, finally, their sense of taste may carry them from a simple meeting of elders to a House of Lords, composed of the finest intellects in all branches of thought and industries. To all this the natives of Africa may aspire in the working out of their own salvation as a people, if some inherent and subtle vice does not arrest their progress.

Now these six categories may be reduced to three

(1) Hearing and Speech may be headed "Science or thought." (2) Smell and Touch may be termed Religion. And (3) Sight and Taste may figure as Order.

Science

In native communities we have the hunter, a brave man, who must not be afraid of the fairies when the whirlwind blows him into the depths of the forest and into their presence, so that he may learn from these departed spirits the cure for certain diseases. This apothecary goes on experimenting and collecting facts and, in this way, is a primitive man of science. He uses his knowledge for the benefit of his family. He may perhaps be called a white magician, at any rate he is the opposite to the impostor or quack who trades on the ignorance of the people and who in this way is a dealer in black magic.

Religion

"Increase and multiply" sums up primitive Religion, which is in this way bound up in the Creator and motherhood. We have noted how the chief duties of the Babalawos or priests are connected with marriage and birth. So long as these priests confine themselves to these moral duties for the benefit of their people they may perhaps be called white magicians, but as soon as they forget their priestly duties and trust to priestcraft they become black magicians.

Law

The ruler who governs his people scientifically and religiously in accordance with the natural and moral laws handed down to him by his ancestors may be called a white magician, but the ruler who attempts to govern his people by means of secret societies that play on their dread of death becomes a dealer in black magic.

True to the most primitive form of government, *i.e.* that of father, mother, son, we conclude that these three material persons symbolise the three great spiritual lines of thought, *i.e.* Science, Religion, and Law. Law then is the offspring of Science and Religion and may be said to be contained in them. We thus arrive at the great "duality" in man.

There remains the Dowager Queen or Iyalode. Iyalode as we have seen is the relict of the departed father and so represents or symbolises the departed spirit. We have further noted that when the father dies the mourners cry out Oro O! Baba O! and by Baba or father we are told they mean the first great father and not the immediate deceased. In this way we are correct in concluding that the Iyalode symbolises the first great founder and spirit of her husband's race.

I now refer my reader to page 237 in *At the Back of the Black Man's Mind*, where the philosophy will be found in table form.

Environment will colour each of these six "estates" in each perfect kingdom, and each "estate" will need many reforms before it is in itself perfect. The Administrator learned in history will now have no difficulty in placing the West Coast African in his exact position in the historical development of civilisation, and can fearlessly help him upward on what he knows to be natural lines and nature colouring. We need fear no danger in being true to nature, for nature in itself is true to the Divine inspiring Will of the Great Father in whom we all believe. Danger arises from the impulsiveness of those whose true instincts have been perverted, and in whom secondary and unnatural instincts have been inculcated by association with abnormal situations, such as slavery, bad living, and a wrong form of education. These unfortunate people, having lost the principles of the foundations of the six estates, think that no form of government is necessary, and imagine that by destroying the divinely inspired "structure," or parts of it, they will in some way benefit. But if we believe that a kingdom is but a conglomerate form of estates, the output of the senses in man, we shall at once realise the imbecility and futility of the endeavours of these ignorant people. A state can gain no more, for instance, from the abolition of its Church or Senate, in however crude and undeveloped a stage these estates may be, than an individual can from the destruction of his senses of smell and taste. Such a mutilated kingdom is doomed to fall back to ruin and death in competition with one that is more sensible and complete.

Conquering or Protecting Powers have enormous responsibilities cast upon them, for it is to them and to their method of government that the safety and welfare of the people is entrusted. They must not destroy, but try to uplift. A study of the condition of the people of the protected states is therefore absolutely necessary.

The people themselves through disobedience may easily cause all the efforts of the best of protecting Governments to come to nought. The people must believe and have faith in "the powers that be," though they have the right to join in the prayer that both plaintiff and defendant, among the Bavili, kneeling and clapping their hands three times, offer to their king who has just given judgment— "May you continue to keep the 'seven' well in hand."

I will now conclude by asking you to glance at the following lists, which may help to make clear the philosophy at the back of the Yoruba's mind.

I am sorry that I cannot give lists of the sacred lands and rivers, trees, omens and animals, as in *At the Back of the Black Man's Mind*, but I think I have gathered sufficient traces of these to prove that at one time such lists did exist. The Yoruba has progressed more rapidly in the race of civilisation than his brother in the Congo, and this symbolic picture of his philosophy is hard now to find in a perfect state of preservation.

226 NIGERIAN STUDIES CHAP.

YORUBA DEVELOPMENT OF CALENDAR.

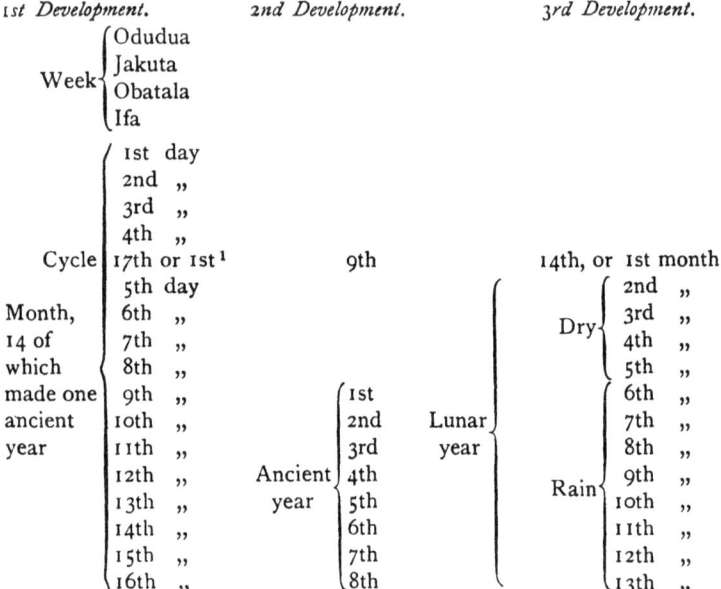

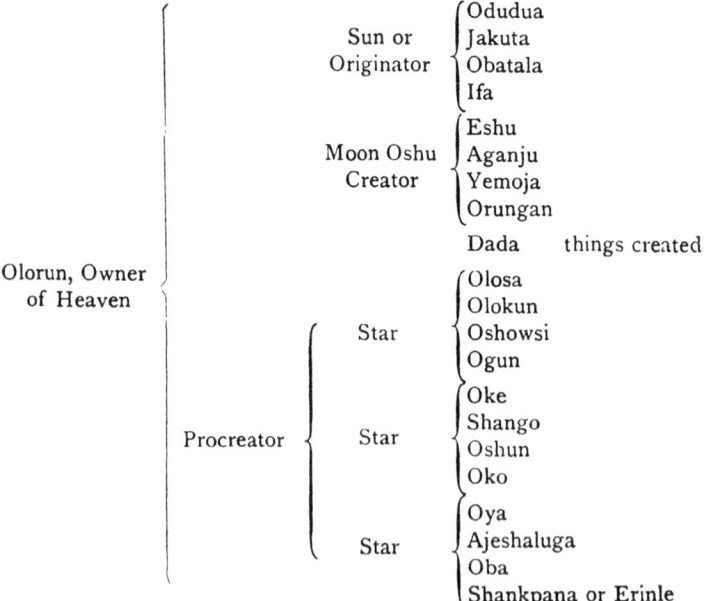

[1] I am here adhering to the formula given by Oliyitan, see list of Odus.

ABEOKUTA HUNTERS' OGBONI OR THE EGBE OLURI ODE.

Iyalode ?	The hunter accused
Akoka or Alake ?	Hunter
Balogun ?	Assistant
Bashorun ?	Hunter
Oyieshile	Assistant
Bi eye oku	Hunter
Ojo	Assistant
Ogbolo	Hunter
	Assistant
	Hunter
	Assistant
	Hunter
	Assistant

THE PRIESTS OF IFA AND THE ODUS.

Priests.	*Odus.*
Oluwo Osi Awo	
Oluwo otun Awo	Orun
Olopon ekeji Awo	
Babalawo	
Babalawo	Odu
Olowo	Ogbe meji
Odofin	Oyeku
Aro	Iwori
The accused	Odin or Edi
Ajigbona	Iroshun
Assistant	Owonrin
Aworo	Obara
Assistant	Okonron
Asarepawo	Oguda
Assistant	Osa
Asawo	Ika
Assistant	Oturupon
Apetebi	Otura
Assistant	Irete
?	Oshe
Assistant	Ofu

228 NIGERIAN STUDIES

THE ARO OR OWE OF THE FARMERS.

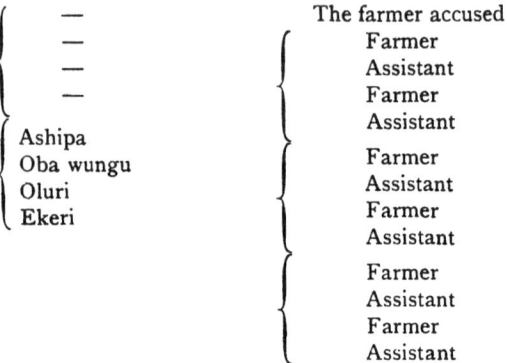

{ Ashipa
  Oba wungu
  Oluri
  Ekeri }

{ —
  —
  —
  — }

{ The farmer accused
  Farmer
  Assistant
  Farmer
  Assistant }

{ Farmer
  Assistant
  Farmer
  Assistant }

{ Farmer
  Assistant
  Farmer
  Assistant }

THE MARKET WOMEN AND PEOPLE'S OGBONI OR THE SENSE COMMON TO ALL.

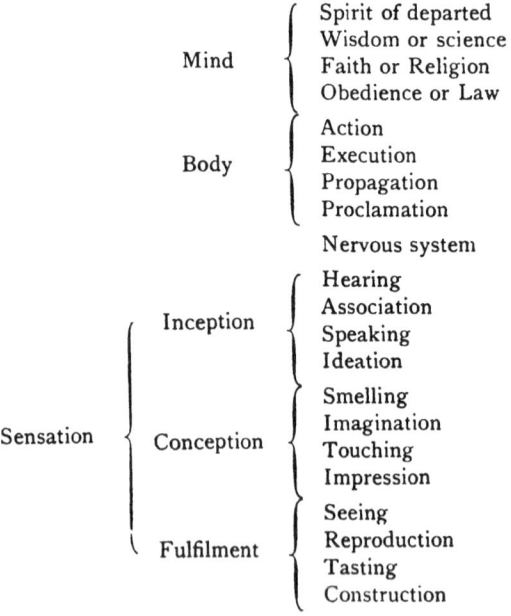

Mind { Spirit of departed
       Wisdom or science
       Faith or Religion
       Obedience or Law }

Body { Action
       Execution
       Propagation
       Proclamation }

Nervous system

Sensation {
  Inception { Hearing
              Association
              Speaking
              Ideation }
  Conception { Smelling
               Imagination
               Touching
               Impression }
  Fulfilment { Seeing
               Reproduction
               Tasting
               Construction }
}

THE KING'S OGBONI.

Native form of Government, of which the Oba is the head
- Executive
  - Iyalode, the Queen Dowager
  - Oba, the King
  - Balogun, the War Chief
  - Bashorun, the Prime Minister
- Legislative
  - President, the Bashorun
  - Akpena, who convenes the meeting
  - Oluwo, the Treasurer
  - Odofin, the Arbitrator
- Council or Ogboni
  - Justice and Life
    - The Plaintiff
    - Lisa, Iwarefa
    - Egbe " Or Assistant
    - Bisa "
    - Egbe "
  - Church and Marriage
    - Bala "
    - Egbe "
    - Asalu "
    - Egbe "
  - Death and Offspring
    - Malukun "
    - Egbe "
    - Ashipa "
    - Egbe "

POSSIBLE DIRECTION OF DEVELOPMENT.

Head of the Church The King	The Court of Equity
The Lord Chancellor The Prime Minister	The Courts of Justice
The Prime Minister The Speaker The Chancellor of Exchequer	The Church
The Lord Chief Justice The People or Nation	The State
	The Commons
	The House of Lords

ADDENDUM

THE SMALL POX GOD.

How Its Priests and Priestesses Ply Their Inhuman Trade.[1]

Suggestions for putting an end to this traffic in human lives.

The method of effecting the cure of the Small Pox disease among the Yorubas was known only to a class of men (priest and priestesses) who make a big trade of the affair by elevating the small pox into a god. One tradition states that Shoponna (Small Pox) was a very wicked boy who often excited great commotions in his town. On one occasion after he had beaten to death several of his townspeople, he was taken by his parents and sold to a native doctor who taught him the use of very bad and poisonous drugs.

With these he effected the death of most of his fellow citizens. No one dared mourn the death of these victims but will suffer deprivation of his house and property; and worse still the relative of the deceased while in that house of mourning has to pay Shoponna and his master a congratulatory visit thanking them for having claimed a victim from their midst. Hence the small pox is ofter termed *Alapadupe* (a man who kills and is thanked for the killing). After his death the shoponna was deified and worshipped.

The following materials can be found in the house of every small pox priest or priestess as emblems of the presence of this god:—1. A calabash containing some portion or portions of the carcase of a small pox victim such as the elbow right on to the palm of the hand; and the ankle right on to the palm of the foot. 2. A pot containing some black liquid which is made up of water collected from the body of the corpse or that with which the deceased was washed when alive. 3. A small vessel of black powder compounded from the trash of the small pox after it is dried up. It is the

[1] From *The Nigerian Chronicle*, February 25, 1910.

water or powder that is always thrown during night time in front of the houses of individuals who are spotted: the inmates inhale the germs during the day when at work or at play and in this way the infection is caught on. Immediately the rash is seen on any one a priest or priestess is to attend on him and in nine cases out of ten helps to spread the disease rather than check it. It is more to his or her interest to do this, for apart from the heavy amount he receives for medical attendance, he claims for himself *all* the personal effects of his patient in case he succumbs.

These priests do not bury the dead but throw the corpses into the bush to be devoured either by carrions or pigs who sometimes drag the inedible portions into the town and in front of houses. In this way is the disease made to spread and priests drive a very lucrative trade. When a few years ago the Government compelled some people in a hinterland town to bury these corpses, the priest often found it necessary to dig a dozen or more graves daily to await the news of small pox victims.

Unless the Government track these wicked priests to their very recesses in the farms of the Yoruba towns—and there are a great number of them in Abeokuta, Ijebu and Ibadan farms—and burn up their materials and houses of worship, the small pox disease will ever continue its ravages in this quarter of Southern Nigeria. It is not enough to arrest worshippers in large towns like Abeokuta only. Those found there are but the disciples of the real worshippers. Let the Government pursue them into their strongholds in the Egba and other farms, if this epidemic is to be checked. A capitation fee paid to any successful detective under this head, I am sure, will bring the desired end.

ADESOLA.

INDEX

ABEOKUTA, 7, 14, 44, 45, 51, 62, 85, 92, 112, 159, 164, 193, 204
Adesola, 28, 31, 35, 36, 41, 55, 59, 87
Aganju, 97, 100, 101, 226
Agbarigbo, 103, 144
Ajele, 194, 199, 201-204
Ajeshaluga, 101, 102, 143-145, 191, 217, 226
Alafin, 6, 8, 58, 91, 92, 199-201, 204
Alake, 12, 14, 77, 92, 112, 192, 227
Alaketu, 12, 13, 76, 77, 92
Alashe, 22, 23, 104.
Alldridge, T. J., 55, 59
Awnomila. *See* Orunmila

BABALAWO, 2, 26, 46-48, 71, 90, 93, 149, 151, 152, 165, 167, 174, 178, 180, 218, 222, 227
Bale, 17, 199, 201-204, 206-208, 216
Balogun, 15, 61-64, 85, 105, 173, 193, 206, 227, 229
Barbot, 61, 67, 107-109, 132
Bashorun, 61-64, 97, 105, 151, 193, 226, 229
Basuto, 57
Bavili, 58, 69, 82, 85, 120, 157, 191, 210, 213, 225
Bellamy, C. V., 126-129
Bini, 9, 39, 56, 62, 63, 66, 76, 80, 82, 108, 110, 121, 148, 157, 199
Birth, 136, 167, 168
Blacksmith, 125-129, 214
Blyden, Dr. E. W., 156
Bosman, 68, 132, 138, 157, 167
Bull-roarer, 28, 33-53
Burial customs, 28-33, 36, 41-44, 56-58, 176, 189, 219.
Buruku, 71, 79, 102, 219

CALENDAR, 60, 63, 77-80, 100-104, 130-139, 191, 215, 226

Campbell, D. R., 198
Categories, 151, 152, 190, 191, 215, 220-225
Chimpanzee, 34, 35
Circumcision, 167, 168
Colour, 217-219
Cotton, E. P., 170, 197
Crawley, 3
Creation, 17, 18, 74, 83
Crowther, Bishop, 45, 73, 77, 81, 82, 86, 90, 145, 210

DADA, 101, 102, 144, 168, 189, 190, 226
Dahomi, 7
Divination, 148, 149

EGBA, 7, 14, 29, 36, 37, 41, 43, 51, 53, 91, 93, 140, 142, 164, 192, 200, 204, 206
Egbo, 55
Egun, 28, 29, 30, 33, 183
Egungun, 28-33, 36, 54, 56, 58, 104
Eleda, 17, 18, 74, 86, 147
Elegba, 94, 95, 100, 103
Eleko, 28
Elgee, Captain, 24, 25
Ellis, Colonel, 33, 46, 51, 70, 73, 74, 77-79, 81, 86, 87, 95, 98, 101-103, 110, 111, 114, 123, 148-150, 158, 159, 168, 170, 214
Eluku, 55, 56, 58
Erinle, 188-190, 226
Eshu, 25, 26, 77, 78, 93-97, 100-102, 104, 117, 151, 170, 186, 226
Ewaw, 170, 175-188
Execution, 41, 43, 45

FARMING, 130-133, 138-145, 215, 216
Fire, 216
Fishing, 106-114, 133, 198, 211, 212

INDEX

Flood, 114, 115
Food plants, 131, 133, 138, 139
Frazer, J. G., 159, 175

GEORGE, MR., 153
Government, 61, 62, 91, 92, 97, 105, 192-194
Grove (Sacred), 19-22, 25, 150

HADDON, DR., 38
Hartze, H., 55
Hausa States, 11
Healy, J. J. C., 196
History, 6-16
Hunting, 116-123, 198, 213, 214

IBADAN, 8, 43, 51, 159, 162, 188, 200, 201-204
Ibibio, 176
Ifa, 2, 3, 18, 19, 63, 64, 71, 73, 78, 80, 86-97, 100-104, 110, 114, 115, 118, 123, 137, 147-155, 164, 165, 167, 170, 176, 181, 184, 191, 218, 226, 227
Ife, 8, 11, 15, 19, 22-27, 69, 77, 87, 89, 201
Ijebu, 8, 55, 89, 92, 93, 200, 203, 204
Iketu, 8
Ilesha, 8
Ilorin, 8
Initiation Ceremonies, 38-40, 56
Insignia, 192, 193
Iro, 28, 34-36, 104, 172, 173
Iron-working, 125-129

JAKUTA, 12, 17, 63-68, 71-72, 77-79, 97, 99, 101, 124, 137, 138, 169, 206
Johnson, Bishop, 63, 73, 81, 86, 87, 148, 149, 152, 170

KERIBO, 88, 158
Kingsley, Mary, 108

LAGOS, 8-10
Land tenure, 195-208
Leopard, 120, 192
Lishabi, 7, 8

MALU, 38
Market, 80
Marriage, 156-162, 165-167, 175-182, 191, 216
Mbundu, 56
Mohammedanism, 11, 12, 75
Morimi, 22, 23

NIEPOS ARA ORUN, 51
Nkimbi, 53

OBA (Chief), 61-64, 105, 199, 219, 229
Oba (Orisha), 101, 102, 144, 168, 169, 189-191, 219, 226
Obatala, 63, 64, 69, 71, 73, 74, 78, 79, 81-86, 97, 100, 101, 103, 114, 132, 147, 167, 170, 181, 186, 226
Odedaino, 165
Odu, 2, 4, 73, 80, 88-90, 110, 147-152, 191, 226, 227
Odudua, 11, 18, 19, 58, 63, 65, 71, 73-77, 79, 80, 82-84, 87, 96, 97, 99, 101, 104, 111, 115, 147, 170, 172, 173, 186, 214, 226
Ogboni, 32, 34, 37, 40-42, 44, 45, 57, 62, 91, 92, 97, 98, 101, 104, 105, 123, 152, 193, 221, 226-229
Ogun, 19, 78-80, 101, 102, 104, 116-119, 123-125, 136, 144, 153, 169, 171-173, 180, 182, 183, 191, 213, 214, 226
Oja (priestess), 3, 17, 77, 86, 87, 147, 170
Oja, 13
Oke, 101-104, 143, 144, 158, 159, 162, 164, 180, 191, 216, 226
Oko, 101-104, 143, 144, 158, 159, 164, 166, 180, 187, 191, 216, 226
Oliyitan, 2, 71, 78, 91, 93, 149, 191, 226
Oloawon, 39, 40
Olodumare, 83
Oloko, 202
Olokun, 70, 101-103, 110, 111, 113, 144, 180, 190, 210, 212, 226
Olorun, 12, 17, 18, 46, 48, 67, 72, 86, 226
Olosa, 101, 102, 111, 113, 115, 144, 180, 190, 212, 226
Oloyo, 12, 14, 76
Omens, 113, 118, 119
Omonide, 12, 14, 75-77
Oni, 19, 22-25, 27, 39, 77, 87, 90-92
Onile, 202-205
Oranyan, 24, 26, 90, 104, 170
Ore, 19, 21, 22
Orisha, 3, *et passim*
Orishala, 18, 19, 73, 77-79, 81-85, 103, 104, 173, 186
Oro, 28, 29, 33-59, 104, 154, 181, 188
Oru, 13, 14
Orun, 69, 72, 95, 98, 101
Orungan, 69, 97, 98, 100, 101, 115, 210, 226,
Orunmila (Awnomila), 26, 87, 90, 148, 150, 153
Oshowsi, 101, 102, 104, 117, 123-125, 144, 180, 191, 213, 226

Oshu, 94, 95, 101, 151, 213, 226
Oshun, 101–104, 144, 168, 169, 174, 175, 187, 189, 191, 216, 226
Ovia, 39, 40, 56
Oya, 101, 102, 104, 144, 168, 169, 184, 185, 191, 226
Oyo, 7, 76, 89, 91, 93, 126, 169, 170, 199, 200

PARKINSON, J., 46
Pellegrin, Mr., 37, 42, 83, 171, 204
Phillips, Bishop, 87, 110, 148–150
Poro, 55–56
Property, 142
Punch, C., 52

RAINBOW, 217
Rayner, T. C., 196

SACRIFICE, 23, 31, 34, 37, 44, 47–49, 70, 94, 102, 111, 117, 123, 124, 143, 152, 163, 169, 182–188, 194
Saintyves, P., 67
Salt, 140
Secret Societies, 28, 29, 31, 32, 36, 38, 51, 55–57, 122, 123, 143
Senses, 210, 211, 220, 221

Shango, 12, 58, 65, 67, 72, 78, 79, 92, 101–104, 123, 144, 168–173, 181, 185, 189–191, 216, 219, 226
Shankpana, 71, 101, 102, 144, 187, 189–191, 219, 226
Shoremakun, 180
Slaves, 205
Stone, Rev. R. H., 45
Stones, Sacred, 3, 18, 19, 22, 27, 66, 67, 90, 95

TABOO, *see* Ewaw
Tarahumake, 57
Tasso, 56
Thunderbolts, 65, 68, 136–138, 168
Togun, 3, 17, 18, 24, 26, 67, 73, 77, 81, 86
Tucker, Miss, 44
Twins, 35

WESTERMARK, 57
Winds, 65–71

YEMOJA, 65, 71, 78, 79, 97–105, 113–115, 144, 152, 168, 170, 188, 210, 226
Yemuhu, 18, 73, 74, 147
Yoruba States Origin, 10, 12

"Nigerian Studies"

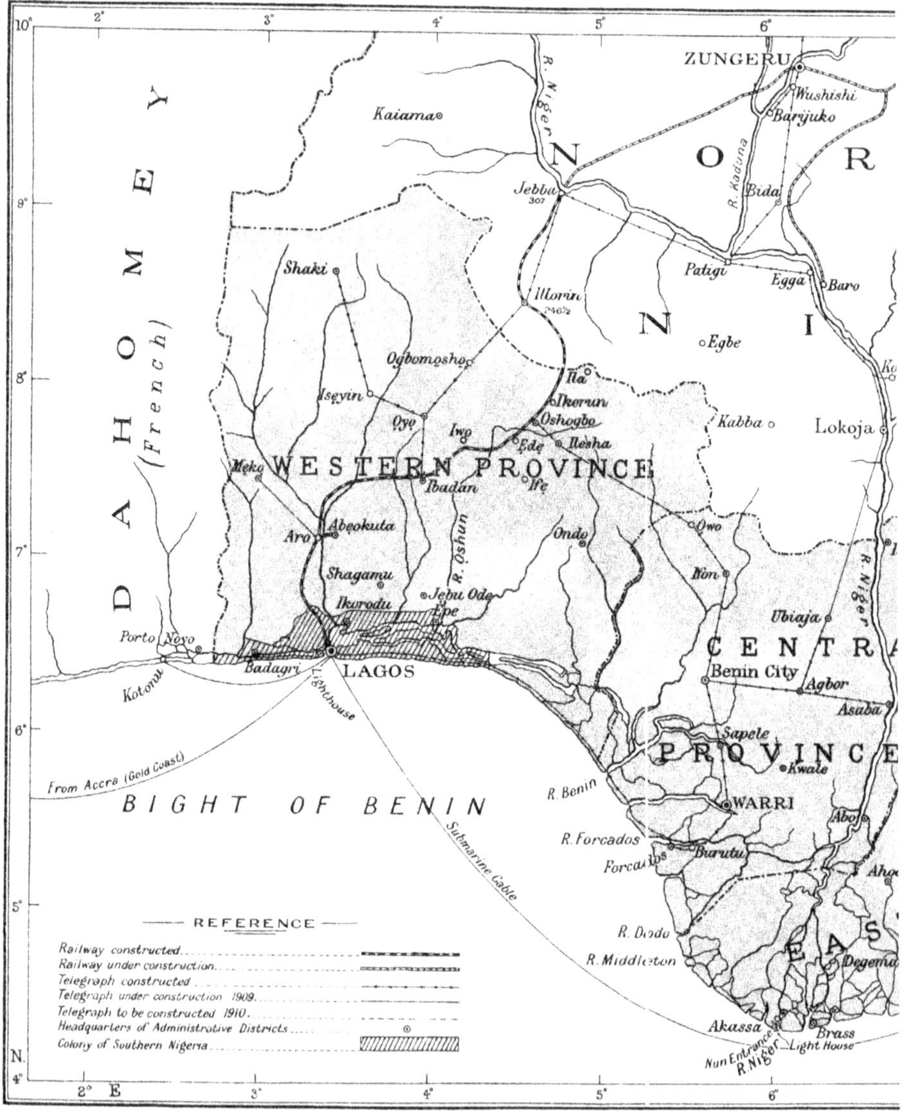

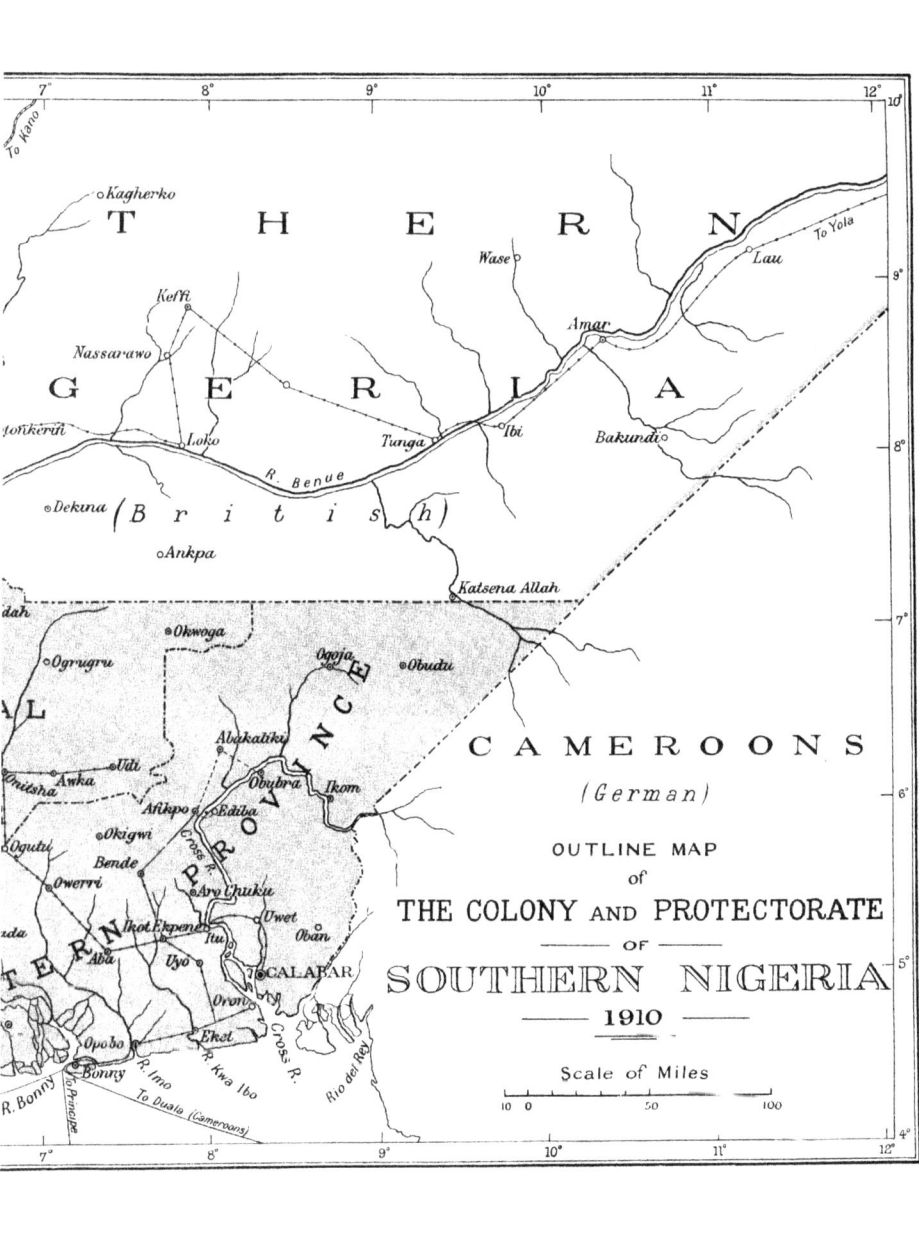

For Product Safety Concerns and Information please contact our EU representative GPSR@taylorandfrancis.com
Taylor & Francis Verlag GmbH, Kaufingerstraße 24, 80331 München, Germany

www.ingramcontent.com/pod-product-compliance
Lightning Source LLC
Chambersburg PA
CBHW071815300426
44116CB00009B/1328